Historically, men have been more likely than women to be guilty of infidelity in a marriage. This is not surprising and is still held as the "typical" expectation when we think about infidelity. However, the number of women engaging in sexual or emotional affairs outside their marriages or relationships has been consistently rising in recent years. According to a 2017 survey by the Institute for Family Studies, approximately 20% of married men reported cheating on their spouses. In the same study, 13% of married women also reported having an extramarital affair. In 2019, there were approximately 62 million married couples in the United States. According to these statistics, over 12 million women and 8 million men may have experienced infidelity by a spouse. These numbers are just in the United States and only represent the married population. The number of men and women affected by infidelity, married and unmarried, throughout the world is far larger.

-Forward-

Why I am Here

Hello, my name is Sean. I am 33 years old and have a full and rich life. I have one of the best families one could ask for, a fantastic network of friends, a successful career and an abundantly active life in Colorado. On the surface, one would say I have it all and they would not be too far off. I cherish so many aspects of my life and my experiences, inclusive of all the highest peaks and the lowest valleys that provide a certain uniqueness to my story.

So, why am I here?

Because, under the surface of a great life, I am a man who has experienced one of the greatest betrayals one can experience in life. I am a man whose wife, partner, confidant and companion chose the cowardly way out and conducted an emotional and physical relationship outside of our marriage and behind my back.

Super Sunday 2019. While most people were perfecting their hot wing recipes, finalizing their last minute "squares" bets with friends and colleagues, or purchasing that new 4K ultra high-definition television that would bring such vividness to the game that you would think it was happening right in your living room, I was lying to everyone I loved.

Let me explain.

On the morning of February 2, 2019, I made a decision that would alter my life forever. I looked at her phone.

For a little while, I had noticed changes in my ex-wife's behavior. It started with just a simple feeling of increased distance and lack of intimacy. What followed was a sense of secrecy and avoidance. Then I noticed other peculiar behaviors, particularly with regards to her attachment to her phone and an odd secrecy to her attitude around it. At first, I thought maybe it was just that she was having private discussions with a close friend who was going through a pregnancy. Perhaps she was entrusted with some sensitive circumstances, feelings or emotions shared by a friend or colleague. Maybe it was an immediate family issue or maybe it was even something fun, like a surprise gift for me. All these speculations seemed to make sense at first. This is because I entrusted this person with my life, my love, my present and my future. I exercised all plausible "benefits of the doubt".

But then it continued, I noticed that many times when we were in the car, an Uber, or just sitting on the couch, she would be typing away with the phone cupped in her hands so close to her face as to not allow me to see what her conversation was about and when I gave the faintest glance over, she would immediately hide the device. I noticed how she was spending much more time behind closed doors in our own home. I attributed this to any and every excuse I could think of and tried to justify it away in my mind.

I could not take it anymore, I had to know. So, on that Saturday morning, while she was sleeping, I glanced at her phone. I was shocked to see that she had not only changed her phone's passcode, but also engaged the facial recognition software. I was her husband and never once had even contemplated invading her privacy as a complete matter of trust until now. This all seemed so odd. But one feature she had not disabled was the lock screen which showed her notifications and previews of the messages she had received overnight.

She had received a WhatsApp message. It was a "heart" emoticon from Matt, a work colleague. My chest pounded and my breathing nearly stopped. For a split second, there was still a reasonable explanation in my head. My ex-wife travelled for work regularly and worked closely on those trips with Matt. In fact, she was leaving for a work trip the next day, Super Sunday. She had probably shared a great idea for that upcoming offsite meeting. Maybe she had offered up a funny anecdote about a project they were working on. Perhaps she had simply given some advice as a good friend or any other number of plausible reasons for receiving a symbol of adoration from Matt.

I felt this way because I knew Matt. I knew Matt's wife. I knew Matt's kids. Not long ago, I was drinking beer with Matt at a company barbeque, doting on my ex-wife and speaking candidly with him about how proud I was of her and how thankful I was for his leadership on her team. I looked up to Matt. He was in a position of leadership and management for my ex-wife's department and I had just entered a similar role in my own career. I saw him as a "good guy", a "family man" and, dare I say it, a friend.

But then I noticed that the preview on her phone screen showed two messages were received. I scrolled to see the other message. What I saw caused the one of the most devastating feelings I have ever experienced in my life.

"Soooooo close (6 big smiley face emoticons)!!!!!! Only 1 more night to go!!! I'm out of my mind excited to see you!!! I keep thinking about being together and cannot contain myself anymore. You are the woman I want to take care of, touch, feel and be with and tomorrow I get to let all those feelings out with you (don't worry, I'll wait until after the SB for some of them [winging face emoticon]). I've missed you so much sweetheart!!! I love you!!!! (6 winking kissing face emoticons)"

I took a picture of the messages with my phone and collapsed onto the couch. I was hyperventilating and uncontrollably shaking. All physical feeling stopped. I was numb and frozen. I knew I could not simply react to what I had seen because I was so far outside of my body. I simply had to get the phone back on the bedside table as if nothing had happened.

Summoning all my will, I walked back to the bedroom to place the phone back on the table. I was shaking so bad that I dropped the phone on my first attempt to replace it. Fearing that the commotion would wake her, I thought, "OH SHIT! Don't wake up! I can't do this! Please, I can't do this!"

Luckily, she did not wake up. I still had time completely to myself to process the feeling that my entire life had just imploded. I placed the phone back and just stared for a few minutes. I stared at her, I stared at the phone and I stared into space. My mind was racing. My thoughts were incoherent and random.

My brain was just filled with phrases ranging from disbelief to rage to uncertainty.

"FUCK YOU!"

"HOW COULD YOU?"

"THIS ISN'T REAL."

"MAYBE THIS IS SOME SORT OF TWISTED JOKE?"

"IT'S OVER!"

"WHAT AM I GOING TO DO?"

"WHAT WILL MY FAMILY THINK?"

"MY LIFE IS OVER."

At this point you might be wondering why I claimed that I was lying to everyone I loved. Surely, I was being lied to, but I was not lying to anybody.

In a ridiculous twist of fate, just a few minutes after discovering the messages on my ex-wife's phone, my brother called. I was so shaky and out of my mind that I went to decline his call and instead accidentally answered. I could not even see straight, and the room was spinning.

What awaited me was a Saturday morning speaker phone call from the east coast with my three and five-year-old nieces laughing and yelling in the background. The type of joyous call that, albeit chaotic, was indicative of an abundance of love, trust and exuberance.

Now in a conversation where I had to fake everything was fine,

I stomached every urge I had to say, "I just found messages on Christy's phone. My wife is cheating on me."

The agony got worse when my brother mentioned that my mother was calling him, and he would try to conference her in!

All I could think of was this devastating revelation and how easy it would be to turn my family's beautiful and joyous Saturday into a day of sorrow, heartbreak and anger. I had this overwhelming urge to broadcast what I knew to people I trusted, because the woman sleeping in the next room was no longer someone I could trust. What a horrible feeling that was. It was only out of respect for our relationship and my fidelity to her, to be true to her in good times and bad, words that ran through my head over and over and over, that I pretended to be fine. Happy, in fact, and excited about our day of ice skating and hanging out with friends. This was the first conversation in which I was now lying to my family, who I so dearly love.

I went for a run to clear my head. I normally went for a long run on Saturday mornings so there was no reason this would indicate anything out of the ordinary. I had resolved to keep this revelation to myself for the time being and to get through the day as planned. I would go for a jog, run a few errands and meet up with friends for ice skating and drinks. I decided to live the lie that everything was okay. I had resolved that I would lie to Christy and my friends, building on the lies I had already told my family.

I just needed one more day. Just one more day of normal. One more day with my life as I knew it. Christy and I had our Saturday. It came and went. The next morning, she left for her work trip, literally and figuratively walking out of my life. That was the moment when I began to feel completely and utterly alone.

So, I ask the question again. Not only of myself, but of anyone reading this as well.

Why are we here?

If you are like me, it is because you are looking for something in the midst of one of the darkest times of your life. Looking for advice, hope, justification, guidance, statistics, really anything that can help you navigate the turmoil you are facing. I know, I am still there and still searching. It has been over a year since that fateful day and I am still learning, adjusting and trying my best every day to own my new reality.

My world no longer consists of the comfortable notions of absolutes. There is a comfort in operating in a space where you can clearly decipher what is right and wrong or see things as black and white. The truth is that navigating the aftermath of an affair plunges you into a different way of dealing with your world. It turns into an uncomfortable mixture of varying hues of gray and intuition versus emotion.

I am writing this because I searched high and low. I Googled almost every keyword and phrase I could think of to see what I could expect on this journey of being a loving and honest man who was betrayed and cheated on. A man who was pushed to the brink of thinking it was something I did to cause this or that I had some sort of blame in her actions.

I wanted to find comfort in documented statistics, professional advice on how to cope and stories of others who have had my experience. I wanted to see the roadmap for how I would rise from the scattered rubble of my life and use it to find meaning, purpose and joy in my reconstructed life.

What I found was scarce information on the male experience of going through a spouse's betrayal. Instead, I found a myriad of information related to the more stereotypical situation, where a wife is recovering from a cheating or abusive husband.

Do not get me wrong, I am ecstatic that those resources exist for those in need of them. But my experience is different, it is unique. However, based on limited statistics, it may not be as unique as I once thought. That is a sad reality, but it is a reality and this book is my small way of not only helping myself, but those who can draw on my experience.

I am Sean and I am an engineer from Colorado. I am not an expert in psychology or any matter of physical or mental health. What I am an expert in is my experience and I am uniquely qualified to share it. I will go as far as to say there is no one more qualified to share my experience than I am. I believe my experience and the journey I have been on since the discovery of my ex-wife's betrayal might possibly help someone who is going through a similar struggle and grasping for answers. I am still going through it, but one thing I have learned is that when you are struggling to survive the aftermath of discovering your partner is having an affair, you are never as alone as you may feel. This is my story of surviving the initial days after discovering Christy's affair. Welcome to my story. I hope it helps with yours.

The names in this narrative are altered out of respect for privacy of those who have shaped my experience. My intent is not to draw attention to those individuals whose actions contribute to my story, but rather, to focus on the story itself.

This book is primarily comprised of reflective commentary on my experience in surviving the immediate aftermath of discovering that I was the victim of infidelity. As such, I have made every attempt to keep the commentary pragmatic and constructive. However, there are times where I reference specific thoughts, internal monologues, and conversations that occurred in those first few days. I feel it is important to present these thoughts and conversations in their unfiltered form as they are a reflection of frantic nature of the survival phase. I advise the reader that some this material may be graphic in nature.

-1-

The Bombshell and Initial Moments

I'm sinking deep, deep inside my mind, thoughts of what I see. Heartbeat keeps time, crescendos with the pain washing over me. I'm frozen now, staring at the screen that ruined everything. I'm shaking now, shaking without end, uncontrollably.

It's like a rising tide in the caverns of my mind. The way out is hard to find. I'm gasping for air. This fear has taken me. The water is getting deep. There's only lonely when gasping for air.

Time's standing still, stiller than the snow falling peacefully. Yet fires rage, burning in my mind, consuming all of me! Tears fill my eyes. I can't see. My lungs have died. I can't scream. Somebody take this from me. Lifelines are out of reach.

It's like a rising tide in the caverns of my mind. The way out is hard to find. I'm gasping for air. This fear has taken me. The water is getting deep. There's only lonely when gasping for air.

I have always been musical. It is a part of my life that was instilled in me at a young age by my parents. My mother could play just about any song in the church hymnal on the piano. Some of my most cherished childhood memories involved singing with her and the local church choir when I was only five or six years old.

My father would talk about the glory days when he could rip on the drums. I have to admit that I have never heard him lay down a "gut busting" percussion fill between a verse and a refrain. However, I know my dad has a serious talent for timing and rhythm based on the many drum solos he played on the steering wheel along to the songs playing on the car radio.

I am so grateful that my parents gave me the gift of music. What I once considered a nuisance of having to sit down for thirty minutes and practice the piano in my youth, morphed into an element of my life that I draw on as a focused escape. For me, music provides clarity and respite, while fueling channelized creative energy which feeds the mind and soul. Music has this ability to intertwine emotion and reason to describe the human experience in a way words alone cannot. Perhaps this is why lyrical poems, sonnets and ballads have provided the clearest expressions throughout history of the most complex human emotion. Love.

In my quest to wrap my mind around the emotions I felt on that fateful Saturday in February 2019, I instinctively turned to writing music. But it was not immediate. I wrote the lyrics that start this chapter nearly nine months after the day I first discovered my ex-wife's affair. In those initial days after discovering my ex-wife's affair, I experienced so many emotions and experiences, many of which I will talk about. But that is something I do not want to just gloss over. It took me almost nine months to not only bring myself to truly contemplate my initial emotions tied to the discovery that my ex-wife had betrayed me and our marriage, but to even begin to understand those emotions.

In retrospect, the truth is that in the face of my devastating discovery, my feelings and actions were more a result of adrenaline than they were about emotion. Discovering my ex-wife's affair initiated something more akin to survival. I know I had emotions swirling, but I could not be emotional. I had to try to be rational in an irrational circumstance.

In one minute, I was a married man who was just simply

concerned and wondering how to get the "spark" back. In the very next moment, I was a man whose past was a lie, whose future was shattered and whose present was instantaneously chaotic. Nothing can prepare you for this moment.

Nothing.

If I had been preparing for this moment, I probably could have blamed myself for not being more proactive in making the changes necessary to avoid its occurrence. I will go as far as to say that if I was prepared for this betrayal, I probably should not have even been married to her in the first place.

A real marriage is so much deeper than just love and commitment. It is about unwavering trust, unquestioning loyalty and a deep faith in your partner's intentions. Sure, troubles can arise, and temptations can creep in, but a true marriage is about knowing beyond a shadow of a doubt that you want the best for your partner, and they want the best for you. The moment before I checked Christy's phone, I was living in that marriage. I was suspicious that she was keeping something from me, and I was concerned. But I believed, as I always had, in my wife's intentions. I had accepted and believed in a "truth" that she would never, ever intentionally be malicious and hurt me.

The collapse of that "truth" that was at the center of my life as a married man is what fueled my survival instinct. Looking back on that Saturday, I cannot really recall my specific feelings about Christy. The lasting mental imprint was more tied to my survival response to a threat and the ensuing fear.

I have often read that humans, from a young age, are conditioned to recognize pain and fear. We are conditioned to not only recognize it after we experience it, but to immediately avoid it when confronted with it again. But if we cannot avoid it, we try to escape, mitigate or fight it, in an effort to survive.

This natural survival response is why I believe the emotions I felt were blurry and hard to process, but the mental and physical responses are so ingrained in me now. I am quite certain that I will never be able to forget the exact surroundings and circumstances of the moments immediately after I found out about her affair.

In the weeks preceding my discovery, Christy had been acting odd and had this obsession with being on her phone. But it was not in the typical way in which most people in our society are glued to their phones. It was very secretive. If we were driving or in an Uber, I would notice her typing away. When I looked over at her, not even at her phone, she would quickly flip it over to conceal the screen. She also had been taking her phone behind closed doors in our own home for extended periods of time. She would disappear into the bathroom with her phone for close to an hour at times.

I wanted to give her the benefit of the doubt. I trusted in that "truth" of believing that my wife would never intentionally hurt me or be malicious towards me. Given this trust, I also did not see the need to infringe on a reasonable expectation of privacy.

However, the night before, Christy and I went on a date night to see a movie together. I suggested we make a night out of it and go to dinner as well. She declined dinner and opted for simply seeing the movie, noting that she had an upcoming work trip that she had to leave for on Sunday, so she would probably need some of the evening to prepare material. After the movie, as we were driving home, I was trying to have a conversation with Christy. I noticed she was "half there" for the conversation and noticed that she was on her phone the entire ride. However, she was holding her phone at an angle at which I could not see what she was doing.

I thought to myself, "What has been so important on her phone that she cannot keep up a twenty-minute conversation with me?" I had a gut instinct that she was being secretive because she really did not want me to see what was on her phone. So, as we went to bed that night, I decided that I would look at her phone while she was still sleeping the next morning if I woke up before her.

The next morning, a Saturday, I woke up and noticed that

Christy was still asleep. Her phone was set on her bedside table. I slowly maneuvered my way out of the bed making every effort to not disturb her. I felt my pulse racing as I pulled the phone off the table and walked out of the room.

I looked at the phone for the first time over a little bar cart that we had near the kitchen. I tried to simply activate the phone from sleep mode, but Christy had apparently enacted a new password and had even enabled the facial recognition identification software to unlock the device. However, she had not disabled the ability to preview notifications on her lock screen. This included notifications for messages she had received while the phone was inactive overnight.

I slid my finger down the glass screen to reveal the preview of a message she had received overnight. I saw the "heart" emoticon from my ex-wife's work superior, Matt. I felt a lump form in my throat. I tried to justify what I had seen in any way I could. But then I saw a second message notification had also come in overnight from Matt. As I revealed the preview text of this second message, suddenly I was unable to take anything more than a shallow breath and sweat began to pool on my forehead.

"Soooooo close (6 big smiley face emoticons)!!!!!! Only 1 more night to go!!! I'm out of my mind excited to see you!!! I keep thinking about being together and cannot contain myself anymore. You are the woman I want to take care of, touch, feel and be with and tomorrow I get to let all those feelings out with you (don't worry, I'll wait until after the SB for some of them [winging face emoticon]). I've missed you so much sweetheart!!! I love you!!!! (6 winking kissing face emoticons)"

An instantaneous malaise overtook me. Fear quickly followed as I realized that I was holding Christy's phone in my hand and she could wake up at any time. I needed to return her phone to the bedside table as soon as possible. I used my phone to take a photo of the messages, as I knew that I would have no choice but to read them over and over and over again in the coming hours, days and weeks.

I knew I had to return her phone to the bedside table. But first, I walked into the bathroom to look in the mirror. I am not sure why. I think it was like a boxer looking at themselves in the mirror before a big fight. It was like a self-dialogue in the form of looking yourself in the eye and telling yourself to be strong in a moment of solitude before the main event. What I saw looking back at me was more likened to a ghost of myself. I noticed my skin was pale, my eyes were bloodshot, my face was sunken, and my body was visibly trembling.

The trembling. That is the most pronounced sensation I remember in those initial moments. There were spells where I would say it was bordering on convulsions.

I walked into the bedroom. I looked at her peacefully sleeping and I felt nothing towards her. No anger, no sorrow, no love. I was in survival mode. My mind was laser focused on the simple, yet seemingly monumental task at hand. Put the phone back exactly where it was and do it quietly without waking her up.

That was my mission in that moment in the interest of surviving to the next task, the next mission. At that moment, I was honestly too busy to be emotional. That may sound completely backwards. Even writing it, I am thinking back to confirm the truth of the statement. I have thought about it a lot. Like I said, it was a moment of being terrified. It left a lasting imprint. I was mentally operating in acute clarity at that moment. Not emotion.

But my body was still physically reacting to the revelation. The hyperventilating and trembling were nearly uncontrollable. It was something I had to overcome in order to complete my mission.

However, the physical reaction proved to be a more powerful force than my mental acuity. I dropped the phone. It hit the corner of the table then bounced off the bed just inches from her face before it landed face down on the carpeted floor. I immediately panicked. In my moment of laser focus, the sound of the phone clambering to the floor came across with the shocking sound of clapping thunder echoing across a canyon. What I heard was deafening.

Apparently, what she heard was barely enough to cause a slight twitch of her nose while she peacefully slept. I picked up the phone. Both hands this time. I managed to gently place it on the table.

Mission accomplished.

Only after this did I let myself start to feel anything. It struck me that I was operating at such an intense level of focus due to situational stress. The mere thought of waking her up when I dropped the phone induced a fear unlike anything I have ever felt before. Meanwhile, she was so relaxed and peacefully sleeping in. At this point, it was past nine o'clock on that Saturday morning.

I thought to myself, "How dare she just sleep there peacefully as my whole world just fell apart?"

Emotions flooded in as I stood over her, sleeping without a care in the world. My mind was littered with phrases ranging from disbelief to rage to uncertainty.

"FUCK YOU!"

"HOW COULD YOU?"

"THIS ISN'T REAL."

"MAYBE THIS IS SOME SORT OF TWISTED JOKE?"

"IT'S OVER!"

"WHAT AM I GOING TO DO?"

"WHAT WILL MY FAMILY THINK?"

"MY LIFE IS OVER."

I had to get out of there. So, I walked out of the bedroom and sank into the couch.

I'm sinking deep, deep inside my mind. Thoughts of what I see.

The life I had created would not let me just escape. I could not just run away. I had a mortgage, a career, a community of friends and family that I would have to navigate. What were previously key elements of a fulfilling and successful life were now restrictions on my ability to just get the hell out of there. To run away and never look back.

I know this sounds harsh. I do not view the good things that make up my life as restrictions anymore, not by a long shot. In fact, those good things became the elements of my life which provided the support and hope that I needed in the days and weeks to come.

However, in those initial moments, my life was the restriction. I could not run. All the access points were closed off as the emotions rushed in. The best descriptor I could think of is being alone in a sea cave as the tide rushes in. There is nothing you can do but wait as the water comes rushing in around you. There is no escape.

It is like a rising tide in the caverns of my mind. The way out is hard to find. I'm gasping for air.

The inevitability of the situation surrounds you and fear wells up around you.

As I sank into that couch, a realization came over me. My life had not changed yet. In this moment, I was still married, my wife was still in the next room with no knowledge of what I knew. My family and friends were going about their lives as if nothing had happened. The world outside the window kept turning with the excited and social hum brought on by an abnormally warm and sunny February day in Colorado. This moment was all mine. The pain and misery in this moment were all mine. All I had to comfort me was the consistent and amplified rhythm of my heartbeat.

Then my phone rang.

-2-

The First Lies

I do not recall the specifics of the conversation. Well, let me clarify. I do not recall exactly what was discussed but I do recall the general topics of discussion. I was sitting on the couch, staring at the blank television screen in front of me. I had not turned it on. In fact, it was more of a mirror than anything. A black mirror in which I could vaguely make out expressions on a silhouetted reflection of myself.

My appearance was remarkably lifeless. Eyes half open and without focus. Mouth opened as if I needed to assist my nose in order to take breaths. My arms were draped by my side and my body was slouched. I was demonstrating the exact opposite posture of the ergonomically correct position for a human to sit.

My phone vibrated in my hand. I was honestly shocked I was even holding onto the thing. It had been dangling in a three-finger grip in my right hand off the edge of the couch. "Grip" is probably too strong of a word. In reality, it was half balanced on my middle and pointer finger while my thumb provided just enough friction to prevent it from slipping out of my now sweating hand. By some miracle, the vibrations did not knock it loose. Rather, the vibration served as a type of wake-up call. An alarm to snap me out of my malaise and thrust me back into reality.

The vibration was the product of an incoming call from my older brother. There was no way I could take the call. I mean even if I had wanted to, how would I? If the sound of my voice did not wake Christy up in the other room, surely the sound of closing a door behind me to go to a private room would be clatter enough.

Even if I did answer, what in the world would I talk about? Whatever I did talk about would probably be in the form of a scratchy, frail voice wrought with the intermittent cracks to hide accompanying tears.

All of this raced through my head as I adjusted my grip to decline the call. To swipe the red phone icon from right to left. However, that grip adjustment produced an unexpected outcome as my thumb dragged from left to right. The timer started. The connection was live.

I quickly ran into an adjacent room and closed the door softly. From there, I scurried into an interior bathroom which connects to that room. This provided an additional level of privacy to stifle any sounds of a conversation from entering the room where Christy was still sleeping. In five minutes, I had gone from curiously looking at my ex-wife's phone to cowering in an interior bathroom to have a conversation with my brother for fear of waking her up.

"Hello", I said in the most secure and stable voice I could cough out.

"Hey Sean!" my brother responded.

He continued, "Hey, let me put you on speaker, the girls want to say hello."

I then heard the pronounced shift in the call's background noise from muffled and muted to the true representation of my brother's house on that Saturday morning.

"Hi Uncle Seanny!" two high-pitched voices proclaimed. Their delivery of the greeting was loud and melodic, like the way an elementary school class greets anyone who walks in the classroom. Why just say hello when you can sing it?

They then began to talk over each other in an effort to explain their exciting Saturday morning activities. I cannot remember exactly what it was about, but I am sure it was something along the lines of a competition for who was making a better pretend pie out of Play-Doh. Inevitably, the competition to impress me turned dramatic and quickly escalated into an argument between them.

"Hold on Sean." my brother said.

Then he put the phone aside to calm the girls down, likely by leveraging a threat to take the Play-Doh away if they did not play nicely. My newest nephew, just a few months old, then joined in on the action with some soft babbling and banging on his highchair.

"Hey Sean!" my sister-in-law yelled towards the phone. I can only imagine she was greeting me over her shoulder as her focus was likely on getting those mushy carrots into my nephew's mouth and not having them flung back at her!

There was nothing abnormal about this call. It was representative of the typical conversation I would have with my brother at the end of a long work week. A Saturday morning marking the start of forty-eight hours of freedom from the grind of life's routine. No emails or meetings. Just cereal, coffee, juice, family, and Play-Doh! It was indicative of a chaotic, yet beautiful symphony of life. A Saturday morning just like every other Saturday morning in that house in Virginia. How envious I was in that moment.

Just as we were about to attempt to squeeze a few words related to an adult conversation into the fold, my brother abruptly interrupted.

"Hey Sean, wait, wait, hold on a second! Mom's calling. I'm going to conference her in!"

"Are you kidding me?" I thought to myself.

Not only was I trying to figure out how to fake it for a few minutes with my brother, but now my mom was joining on the line? This is the woman who is naturally conditioned to see right through me. There is simply no way I can conceal what I had just discovered.

It quickly overwhelmed me that I had a remarkably simple, yet profound choice to make.

If I was to tell anybody in my family about what had happened,

I would immediately be relinquishing my complete control of not only the circumstances of my situation, but also my ability to make an unbiased decision about what I wanted going forward. I was still a married man, and although Christy had totally steamrolled the notion of "being true" to me, I was not ready to accept that yet. Even considering what I had just discovered, I had to put my marriage first.

I heard a subtle click accompanied by an additional source of slight background noise. The conference connection was successful.

"Hey Mom. How's it going?" I greeted my mom.

I feel horrible saying this, but I wanted to find an excuse to end the conversation as quickly as possible. The two other people on the line were living in truth. I was immediately living in guilt, deceit and dishonesty.

Although only for a very brief time, up until this phone call I owned the information I had discovered. Christy was still sleeping, so I had not directly lied to her about knowing or not knowing. At worst, I was simply mitigating the situation with her. Kicking the can down the road if you will. As long as she was still sleeping or if I was not around her, I had no need to lie to her.

But with my brother and my mother, I would have to withhold information. I would only have to lie by omission, but it is still lying to those I love. My mom then asked me the basic open-ended question that kicks off the majority of any adult conversation.

"How are you guys doing?"

Well, there it was, the question I was dreading. My throat closed and my heart sank.

"We're doing well," I answered.

The first lie.

I continued. "We had a great time last night at the movies. Went to see Free Solo. That guy is nuts!"

It then hit me. I had introduced a topic that I could focus on to talk intelligently about. I immediately launched into commentary on what kind of person could climb a sheer wall, thousands of feet in height, without any ropes or safety gear. I launched into the myriad of potential deadly scenarios and "What-ifs" that were beyond the control of a human hanging off a slab of granite two-thousand feet in the air.

"I mean, what if a bird flew past and startled him? What if an insect landed on his face? What if he got a simple itch and flinched? What if the finger thin rock grip cracked and flaked off the wall?"

This discussion of conditions under which Alex Honnold scaled El Capitan in Yosemite National Park, provided the exact conversational fodder I needed in that moment.

Once my theatrical review ran its course, my brother asked about what Christy and I had planned for the day. I responded that I was probably going to go for a run and then we were going to meet some friends for ice skating and drinks afterwards. I mentioned that Christy had to run to the store to pick up some last-minute supplies for her work trip and pack before her flight on Sunday morning. As I listed the litany of items that could fill the day's itinerary, I began to see a full calendar as a welcome reprieve.

For anyone who has ever been on a conference call, either for work or for personal conversation, it is shocking how the dynamics of group conversation breakdown when you eliminate facial expression and body language.

Soon the conversation became a broken and choppy chorus of half-phrases as we each simultaneously attempted to fill the voids of silence between spoken thought. I used that as my opportunity to exit the discussion.

"Okay, it's getting a little hard to hear you. I will talk to you later. Have a great day! Love you!"

My momentary plunge into a world of deceit was over. I resolved that I would avoid phone calls for the rest of the day.

Now it was time to get out of the condo before Christy woke up.

My situation had not changed. I still had not even begun to process any coherent thoughts about how I would respond to her. If I wanted more time to think about it, I had to get out of the condo. Every minute I was still there was a game of Russian roulette. At any minute, the bedroom door could swing open with Christy walking toward me with a "Good Morning" and a hug. There was no way I was ready to navigate that.

I grabbed whatever running clothes I could find and threw on my Brooks running shoes as quickly as possible. It was not out of the ordinary for me to go on an hour plus distance run on Saturday mornings. So, I left the condo and did precisely that.

-3-

One Foot in Front of the Other

I barreled down the stairs of my condo building and bolted out of the main door. Typically, I would pause there to start my music and make sure my headphones were working properly. On any ordinary day, I would stand there and wait for a full GPS signal on my activity tracker because I wanted to make sure that every hundredth of a mile was accounted for. But that was not the case on that Saturday morning.

On that day, I was acutely aware that my pre-run routine was within view of several of the windows of my condo. I did not get all the way out the door just to be spotted and summoned back into the house to say good morning to the half-asleep source of my despair.

I immediately darted down the sidewalk and rounded the corner of the building. I was now out of the line of sight from my condo, but still needed more distance to feel secure. I ran for two blocks before I finally took a pause and gathered my thoughts. I had not even thought about how far I would run or where I would go. Eventually I would have to come back, but when? How long could I get away with being out before it would seem suspicious? Also, I needed to communicate that I was out for a run as to not raise suspicion that something was not right.

I quickly sent a text to Christy. "Hey, heading out for a long run, be back a bit later."

I decided that an hour and a half would be a reasonable time for me to be away. I also decided that I would actually use the time to run. I needed to exert the pent-up adrenaline that had been building inside of me. I also needed to think.

A discovery I had made when I was studying engineering in college was that a run around the park was quite effective in providing clear thought to focus on a problem that I was struggling with. Nine times out of ten, I would leave my dorm room after hours of deliberation only to return forty-five minutes later with the solution clearly defined in my mind.

In this case, I had given myself ninety minutes to determine what my next steps would be. I scrolled through my playlist history past the selections that typically would provide the musical background for my runs. I did not need my typical fast paced, lyrical montage of songs meant to drive performance. Rather, I needed something deliberate, thought provoking and, most importantly, without lyrics so I could focus. I chose a playlist that I typically play while I am at work, "Epic Film Scores." How appropriate? I needed a soundtrack to frame and gather my thoughts in the drama that was now engulfing my life. Some of the greatest movie soundtracks of all time ought to do the trick. I pressed play and I was off. One foot in front of the other for the next ninety minutes.

My destination was Washington Park, locally known as "Wash Park," in Denver. Wash Park is about three miles from where I lived. Once I arrived there, I could run a loop around the park before heading back to the condo. As I exited the streets of my local neighborhood, I started thinking about the logistics of the next twenty-four hours.

As was the theme of the message that Matt had sent to Christy, the next day was Super Sunday and Christy was heading on a work trip to Florida. There she would meet Matt for their week of meetings, conferences and yes, apparently their passionate affair as well.

Christy had mentioned the night before that she needed to

print some photos and pick up some items from a local department store before her trip. After she mentioned this, I said I would go with her as I had a few items I wanted to pick up as well. We were going to have to get that done before the early afternoon, because we were scheduled to meet up with a few friends for the evening for a social event.

It was an event that I had been looking forward to for a while. A bunch of our local friends were meeting at our neighborhood brewery before heading out to a nearby mountain lake for some ice skating. After that, the plan was to continue the festivities back in Denver with some pizza and bar hopping.

It then dawned on me that the only one-on-one time I really had with Christy on that day would be the trip to the department store. The rest of the day would all be in a group setting. If I needed to, I could use the afternoon and evening's festivities to avoid Christy in a reasonably explainable manner. I could just pour myself into interesting conversations and anecdotes with friends. I could partake in the day as if nothing were wrong right in front of Christy. I could hide from her in plain sight.

Once I had thought through the rest of the day's itinerary in this logical and methodical manner, I began to contemplate if this was the approach I wanted to take. My options were to either partake in the predetermined activities of the day and withhold what I knew or confront Christy as soon as I got back to the condo.

If I confronted her, I would immediately be thrust into a dizzying list of logistical and emotional conundrums. Would I tell her to leave and if so, where would she go and for how long? Would I simply state what I discovered and walk out? Would she get defensive and combative? Then the most realistic and frightening scenario came into focus. What if I stated what I knew and then immediately had no idea what to do?

It was that last question that raced through my mind and overwhelmed me. I knew that confronting her today may stop her from making the trip, possibly stopping a physical affair before it happened. As far as I knew at that point, Christy and Matt's relationship had not yet gone any further than romantic feelings and emotions. This was a very naive thought, given the nature of the texts I had discovered, but I was in survival mode. I was not going to discount any possibility the provided some hope of recovery at this point, no matter how unlikely it may seem to the outside observer.

If I did not confront her, I would have to watch her go on the trip which was sure to lead to a complete emotional and physical expression of their affair. It was at that point I started thinking, "What does it matter?"

It was an honest question. If they were already "in love" with each other, did it really matter if a physical relationship had developed yet? Did it really matter if I stopped the physical relationship? It all hurt. It was all a demonstration of her exploitation of my trust. Regardless of the specific details of the affair, it was still life shattering. It was still a most vile betrayal of our marriage and promise to each other.

As I continued my trek around the interior paved loop of the park, my footsteps provided a consistent metronome keeping time for my thoughts. I took a moment to get out of my head and drink in the scenery around me. It was what they call a "bluebird" day in Colorado where the sunshine was brilliant and there was not a cloud in the sky.

On that winter morning, there was a stark juxtaposition between the barren nature of the leafless trees and the vibrant atmosphere brought on by an abnormally warm and sunny February morning. Throngs of people were out enjoying the opportunity to soak in the sun. The Rocky Mountains showcased a recent alpine snowstorm and gleamed in the distance in all their majesty. There was so much beauty around me. There was so much beauty in my life.

It was in that moment of perspective that I decided I wanted one more day of "normal". This decision was accompanied by an immediate wave of relief. Even if it were only temporary, it would provide the opportunity to have more time to gather my thoughts. Yes, it meant that Christy would leave for her work trip and continue her relationship with Matt unencumbered by my knowledge. But because I had resolved that the extent of the relationship did not hurt as much as the fact the relationship existed at all, this strategy allowed me time for constructive thought. I began to see her trip as more of an opportunity for clarity of thought than a source of stress and anxiety.

But do not get me wrong. There was still severe stress and anxiety over what was happening. All this strategy did was allow me to kick the proverbial can down the road for a few days. More than anything, it just gave me a way to get through the rest of the day with a plan. I did not have to wing it. I could control how and when I wanted to divulge the information I knew. I mean, she apparently had no problem keeping an outside relationship from me. Surely, I could keep my knowledge of her deceit from her for at least a day!

My whole plan for getting through the day hinged on the ability to join up with friends later that afternoon. I could hopefully act as if I did not know anything by successfully deflecting my attention to others. I do not think my friends truly will ever understand how much I was relying on them that day. How grateful I was for them.

All the sudden it dawned on me though. This beautiful, sunny, warm day actually posed a threat. Our plans with friends were centered around driving up to the small mountain town of Evergreen, Colorado to go ice skating on the popular Lake Evergreen. The reality was that the Denver area had experienced several warm and sunny days in a row. I immediately stopped running in the middle of the park and whipped out my phone to check that Lake Evergreen was still open for ice skating.

A digital banner stretched across the homepage for the Lake Evergreen website. "Sorry, due to unseasonably warm weather, Lake Evergreen will be closed for ice skating until further notice. Please check back for updates."

My throat became dry and my chest heavy. I immediately sent a text message to my friend, Monica, who was organizing the event.

"Hey Monica, so it looks like Lake Evergreen is closed. Any alternate thoughts?"

I was careful to send a nonchalant sounding text that conveyed a feeling of disappointment as opposed to a tone of sheer desperation that we needed to come up with a different plan to get the crew together, and we needed to come up with it fast!

I paced back and forth along the shore of the lake in the center of the park. I checked my phone relentlessly for a reply. I must have checked it at least once every ten seconds. I am not sure why, as my notification volume was both on high and the vibration mode was on. I guess I just did not want to miss the reply. In that moment of desperation, I also probably thought as though I could summon a response by incessantly checking for one. One minute, two minutes, three minutes! Come on, when will this torture end?

Finally, after an agonizing ten minutes my phone buzzed, and the message alert tone rang.

Monica responded back "Yeah. Saw that this morning. Bummer!"

She continued, "I checked the rink downtown on 16th street and that seems to be open. How about we just meet at the brewery as planned and head down there afterwards!? Bonus, no one will have to drive!"

She then offered to message the group to explain the revised plan. I was filled with such immense gratitude.

"Sweet! See you guys later!" I responded.

With that the plans for the day were secure. Apart from the trip to the department store, I would be able to use a group setting to get through the rest of the day. If I could just get through today, I would have six days while Christy was on her work trip to gather my thoughts and plan my response to this crisis. As devastated as I was, I felt as if I had struck a bit of fortune.

My biggest challenge now was keeping my emotions and expressions in check for the next twenty-four hours. That was totally under my control. Surely, I could swallow all my feelings and pretend for one day. I had secured my one more day of "normal." I briskly walked back to the main path in the park, changed my music from movie scores to my typical fast paced running playlist and started striding towards home.

-4-

The Performance Begins

It was around 10:30 AM when my run home was coming to an end. Since I had resolved to have my one more day of "normal" while pacing along the lake in Wash Park, I tried to get back to my normal state of mind. I had turned on my "go to" up-tempo running playlist, a montage of songs picked more for their fast-paced beat than their ability to provoke emotion or thought. "Izzo / In the End," off the 2000's Collision Course collaboration album by Jay-Z and Linkin Park brought me down the home stretch. I have had that album in my running mix ever since it came out when I was in college and it still pumps me up every time!

I finished my run about two blocks from my condo. From there I would walk back to my condo like I usually do. The walk would give me a chance to catch my breath and take in the neighborhood buzz of the day. Where my run came to an end was right outside a local sports bar. Because of the exemplary weather, there were hardly anybody inside, but the patio was packed with people enjoying a "boozy brunch."

The outside temperature alone probably would have still been a bit too chilly for people to choose the patio over the inside dining room, but the brilliant, warm Colorado sun was making up for that in spades. People were enjoying the fortunate occurrence that one of the best weather days of the winter fell on a Saturday. Smiles were wide, the food was delicious, and the drinks were flowing. What a great day to be alive.

The walk home gave me the opportunity to observe the world

around me and prepare to act the way I normally would on a day such as this. What an odd state of mind. But it was the state of mind I was going to have to embrace to get through the day. Like an actor getting ready for a live theatrical or television performance, I had to get into character. The morning's discovery had sent my mental state so askew, that I needed that two-block walk to get back into character. To "act" like myself again.

I re-entered the condo building and climbed the stairs to my unit. Christy had not responded to my earlier text, so I really was not sure if she was awake yet or not. Ironically, as I stood outside the door, I really hoped she was awake. I was in character and ready for my performance. What a letdown it would have been to walk into a quiet house with her still sleeping. How difficult would it be to put the mental fortitude I had built up on hold? The wheels were in motion now.

"She better be awake" I thought.

I felt like I was in a place of temporary control of the situation. How unfair it would be if she also took that away from me that morning.

I opened the unit door.

"How was your run?" Christy's voice proclaimed as I walked across the threshold. A sense of relief washed over me. The performance was ready to begin.

"Hey! Good morning," I responded. I was still focused on taking the key out of the door. I had yet to actually see her.

I continued, "The run was great! Went for a nice, long one down to Wash. So many people are out, it is absolutely beautiful outside!"

It was during that statement in which I caught my first glimpse of her awake that morning. It looked like she had just awoken. The coffee machine appeared to be early in its daily operation with the first drips hitting the bottom of the pot. She was still yawning, and her eyes were struggling to become fully open as they adjusted to the brilliant sunlight flooding in through the windows.

So far so good. My performance was working.

"How did you sleep?" I asked.

She had been sleeping in until this late morning hour for quite some time now. It had been a source of frustration for me as of late. It seemed like every week we would talk all week about how we would embark on some great weekend Colorado adventure only for her to claim she was too tired at the last minute and sleep half of Saturday away. In fact, on multiple weekends preceding this one, every Friday afternoon seemed to be marked by a grand plan to beat the ski crowds by heading up to the mountains early the next morning. The reality was we were almost always still in the condo on each subsequent Saturday until noon. Therefore, her response was one I had gotten used to recently.

"I slept okay," She responded. "It felt good to sleep in, but I really just haven't been sleeping that well lately."

I knew she had not been sleeping very well recently. I had been desperately trying to figure out how I could help in recent months to take away some stress from her life. I thought this might have allowed her to get more productive and peaceful rest. She had always claimed to be particularly stressed about work, so I tried to take on most of the other marital and household duties, on top of having my own stressful job. I also had been trying to keep myself in shape. Running, lifting, eating well. I had been trying to be my best self for her.

In fact, for quite some time, I honestly had an animosity brewing in me. I felt as if I was putting effort into every aspect of my life and being extremely accommodating of protecting her wellbeing and stress levels. This, as it turned out, was part of the catalyst that she claims helped drive her actions, but more on that later.

But now her typical answer regarding the quality of her sleep made absolute sense. It gave me a little solace that a small part of her cared, at least on a subconscious level which affected her sleeping patterns, about what she was doing to me.

A thought quickly crossed my mind. "Well, it serves you right that you can't sleep well. I'm actually surprised you can even sleep at all, or keep food down, or look me in the eye, for that matter."

I started to feel my mind spiraling and quickly realized I needed to stop. Projecting how I would attempt to live with myself if the shoe were on the other foot, would be disastrous for my strategy to get through the day.

The truth is, I have absolutely no idea how I would be able to live with betraying my spouse. I do not know how I would be able to live the double life it requires. How stressful and riddled with anxiety that experience would be. There would be a time in my process of coping with her betrayal where I would attempt to understand her ability to live this double life. However, I absolutely could not get sucked into that rabbit hole right now.

"Snap out of it!" I thought to myself.

Back into character.

I responded with forced empathy towards her. "Oh, I'm sorry to hear that. You have been working so hard lately, and I know you have been scrambling to try and get everything ready for your trip. How are you feeling about the trip?"

I could not help myself. Sure, it was manipulative, but I felt like the tank supplying my mental and emotional fortitude needed some fuel if I was going to keep up my performance for the day. I wanted to see her tell me about how she was feeling about her upcoming travel. I wanted to see the nonchalant nature in which she would look me in the eye and tell me how it was just another humdrum business trip that she felt lukewarm about. Could she hide her excitement that all her stresses would surely disappear as soon as her gaze landed on Matt? Their work trip was taking them to sunny Florida near the beach in February. How romantic? She must have been excited.

It then dawned on me that the subject meeting of this upcoming work trip only lasted from Sunday to Wednesday. However, Christy had asked me about two months earlier when she was planning this trip if I would not mind if she extended the trip by a few days. At that time, she noted that the meeting was near the beach and she wanted to take advantage of the opportunity to relax by a beach for a few days. When she had asked me this, I said of course and thought that it made complete sense. I was sincerely interested in my ex-wife's wellbeing and happiness.

This mental revelation ripped through my consciousness and caused a clenching shudder through my body. It dawned on me that this must not be a new relationship. This must have been going on for at least two months. When Christy asked me if she could spend a few extra days at the beach in Florida, what she was really asking was if she could schedule a romantic getaway with Matt, her boyfriend and incredible love. She made that request from a place of utter and complete deception. I obliged from a place of love and trust. I felt like such a fool.

To my inquiry about her feelings regarding her work trip, she responded, "I'm feeling okay about it. I feel like the team is ready but we're going to have to get organized quickly when we get there tomorrow, which won't be easy since all of the guys will probably be wrapped up in trying to watch the game."

She continued, "What time are we meeting everybody today? We should probably head over to the store pretty soon. I need to print those photos for the 'living room' theme we are using to facilitate the meetings."

I responded that everyone was getting together at the local brewery around two o'clock in the afternoon before heading down to the rink off 16th Street. I further explained that the plans had to be altered because of the warm weather's impact on Evergreen Lake.

"That probably works better for me anyway," She said. "I

haven't begun to pack yet for my trip and my flight is early tomorrow. I need to be at DIA before 6:30 tomorrow morning."

If I was pulling my weight as an actor at that moment, she must have felt like she was putting on a performance worthy of an Oscar. Her responses gave me the fuel I needed to continue my one-day deception. I was hiding behind my "character" to veil the rage, turmoil and sadness that was bubbling up within me. I still knew who I was under the facade I was creating. Apparently, she had become fairly skilled in her ability to completely immerse herself in her "character."

She had explored her fantasy to such a degree that it had become a second reality for her. She had developed an immense skill in the art of deception. She could live in one reality in one moment, then flip to her other reality at a whim. In this battle of deception, I was punching way above my weight class, but I was in the fight. A most unfortunate fight.

"Okay, I'm going to grab a shower, then I should be ready to go," Christy announced as she finished her cup of coffee.

"Sounds good, I'll do the same," I responded in kind.

A half hour later, we were heading out the door of the condo, embarking on our trip to the department store.

-5-

The Errand

I do not know if I had really thought about the logistics of our trip to the department store and that it required me to be trapped in a car with Christy for an extended period of time. We were heading to the Walmart in Wheat Ridge off Interstate 70 just west of Denver. I had not been to this particular Walmart before. I am honestly not exactly sure why Christy picked it. All she needed was to print some photographs and pick up a couple "Welcome" mats to create the living room motif for her upcoming meeting. As for me, I just needed some new body wash and shampoo. There was a myriad of other stores in Denver that would have been sufficient for our needs. But alas, we were in the car and on our way to Wheat Ridge.

It was a seventeen-minute drive each way from the store. The fact that I know that it was exactly seventeen minutes probably gives some insight into the agony of every grueling moment. Roundtrip, I would be stuck in the car with her for thirty-four minutes total.

What in the world was I supposed to talk about for more than a half an hour? You know, other than "Hey, so funny story. This morning I looked at your phone and found out that you are cheating on me. Now you say something as there are sixteen minutes left in this car ride and I just wanted to pass the time with some light conversation."

Obviously, I could not talk about the one thing that was racing back and forth in my mind. Also, I mentioned I am an engineer, right? So, you can probably take an educated guess as to my level of comfort with, and limit to, small talk. But it is not like small talk would have really been useful anyway. I mean, anybody who has been in a relationship longer than a week knows that conversation based on small talk might as well come with a giant billboard stating, "THERE IS SOMETHING ON MY MIND THAT YOU SHOULD PROBABLY ASK ME ABOUT!"

I resolved to hide behind the songs on the car radio. A brilliant idea. I immediately hit the preset button for the local Top 40 Hits station. To my delight the latest commercial break was ending with the glorious announcement, "Now let's get back to the music!" Crisis averted.

The likes of Pitbull, L.M.F.A.O and Sam Hunt filled the airways. Nothing too serious and it was the perfect soundtrack for passing time. I cruised down I-70 and each song provided a three to four-minute checkpoint on the race to get to the Walmart finish line and get the hell out of this prison on four wheels.

To keep from any chance that Christy would attempt to hold my hand during the drive, I had primarily been driving with my right hand at the top of the steering wheel. I do usually drive with my left hand at "12 o'clock" and my right arm resting on the center console, but I thought this small departure from normal would not be too obvious.

It is important to note that, at this point, a mere two hours after learning of her affair, I was overthinking everything. What probably did not even garner a second thought from Christy was a glaring departure from the ordinary in my mind. The survival mode was making me hyper vigilant.

"A mile from the exit, almost there," I thought to myself with a sense of relief.

However, just as I allowed myself to relax, "Say Something" by A Great Big World and Christina Aguilera began to play on the radio. If you do not know this song, go take a listen. It is actually relevant and therapeutic if you are facing the potential end of a relationship and need to feel.

With its evenly spaced and haunting piano chords that provide the intro to the song, the song pierced through the muffled sound of the car tires humming on the pavement.

A voice begins, "Say something, I'm giving up on you." As the song continues, the lyrics became more piercing and the tension builds.

I recall that Christy seemed to be looking out the window a lot and I thought I could hear her sniffling. I began to wonder if she might possibly be seeing through my act and realizing that our life as we knew it was coming to an end. Perhaps, she was not seeing through me, but she was just reckoning with her choices in her own mind. Maybe she was understanding that those choices were coming to a crescendo that was leading to a fundamental change in both of our lives, regardless of what I now knew. I just do not know what specifically was going through her head, but what I do know is the compelling emotion in that song was influencing her as well.

The despair emoted by the vocalists on the radio continued to build towards the song's apex. The music engulfed the car as the singers formed a duet.

"And I will swallow my pride. You're the one that I love, and I'm saying goodbye."

These lyrics cut through me in that moment. They brought into focus the history of our relationship. In the last few months, I had been wondering how to get us out of the funk we were experiencing. How had I let our relationship, our marriage, get to this point? Now it had crossed beyond a point of no return and all I could do was focus on surviving the discovery of Christy's affair.

But things were not always like this. There were great times. Amazing times, in fact. What had we done to let those great times slip through our grasps? It seemed like we had just operated under the assumption that everything would be okay someday, but without taking the sometimes uncomfortable, yet necessary, actions to make it so. It was like we were both watching this ball slowly roll off a table. Because it is slow, you have time. So, you look at each other to see which one will reach out and stop the ball first before it gets to the edge.

I wonder what would have happened if the ball was flung across the table? I have to believe that we both would have acted out of instinct to reach out and grab it before it crashed to the floor. We should have had real arguments and real fights along the way. We should have experienced the feeling of truly pissing each other off to the point of instinctively reaching out to mend our relationship before it broke. Instead, we danced around each other's feelings and let little things build and build and build. Now here we were with our relationship shattered in pieces around us.

The song continues with the vocalist pleading to each other, "Say something, I'm giving up on you, and I'm sorry that I couldn't get to you, and anywhere, I would have followed you. Oh say something, I'm giving up on you."

They are wrenching lyrics and so indicative of the truth that you do not just "flip a switch" on love and a deep relationship to turn it on and off. Prior to my discovery, I had known people who have gone through divorce. I had heard it likened to a death as a relatable event to make it explainable for those who have not experienced it themselves. This metaphor, I believe, is an attempt to provide comfort and understanding to not only the recipient of the metaphor, but also the person delivering it.

The truth is that I learned through my story that the finality and uncontrollable nature of death is not comparable to what I was going through. Death is "black and white" in its finality and is generally out of our control. My experience was closer to the sentiment of the song that was resonating through the car. It was more indicative of a sinking ship where we concentrated all our effort on bailing out water rather than taking the deep dive in the dark to plug the leak. Well today the ship went under and my survival was based on my ability to tread water long enough for a lifeline.

That song accompanied us all the way to the end of our journey in the Walmart parking lot. I found a spot only a short walking distance from the entrance. Without saying a word, or even so much as looking at each other, we each got out of the car and headed towards the store. The only words either of us said to each other came when we were walking behind a car getting ready to back out of its spot. The brake lights glowed red with the bright white reverse indicator lights following shortly thereafter.

"Heads up," I instinctively uttered towards Christy as I touched her arm to get her attention. In the midst of all I had discovered about her deceit, I was still as protective of her as I had always been. Again, it is not just a light switch you can flip.

We walked into the Walmart. Christy simply peered straight ahead and let me know that she was going to go to the photo printing center first and then pick up the doormats on the way out of the store. Like just about every other Walmart, the photo center is all the way in the back of the store near the electronics and televisions. I told her that I would pick up some of the items I needed and then meet her back by the photo center afterwards.

Yes, I had some personal items to pick up elsewhere in the store, but my stomach was also a wreck. I may have been able to hide what was tearing me up inside, but my gastrointestinal system did not have the same ability. I started to feel clammy as my stomach turned over and over. The queasiness turned into more shaking and shivering. I had to get control. I walked into the bathroom and straight into a stall where I proceeded to throw up the only thing I had ingested that morning, a single cup of coffee.

Clearing the contents of my stomach provided some temporary relief and allowed me to gather myself. Once I had cleaned myself up, I began to feel semi-normal again. I walked out of the bathroom towards the personal care section of the store to pick up some body wash and other personal items.

After procuring what I needed, I headed over towards the photo center. As I was approaching the book section between electronics and the photo center, I caught a glimpse of her and the self-printing photo terminal where she was working from. She was completely occupied by her task and her back was to me. I noticed that from my vantage point I could see what she was printing.

Again, she was trying to replicate a "living room" theme for her work trip meeting. She was trying to set a scene that was filled with framed personal photos. Mostly, the images that flashed across the screen were landscape photos and pictures of her team. I suppose this was meant to be reminiscent of vacation memories and family portraits that you would find covering the walls of a quintessential American living room.

Then I thought to myself, "She doesn't know I'm standing behind her. I wonder if she is also printing some romantic photos of her and Matt for herself. Is she that bold? She probably already thinks that I have not noticed anything yet and I'm probably too blind or too dumb at this point to figure it out."

The waves of a new feeling were starting to wash over me.

"How could I have missed this?"

I had been so preoccupied to this point with keeping my emotions and actions in check to retain some control over the situation. However, it is only a matter of time before you begin to have this new, all-consuming thought.

"There must have been something I missed."

I knew I had to compartmentalize this fledgling thought process for the time being. I would have plenty of time to myself over the next week to go over the last few months with a fine-toothed comb. The circumstances around every conversation, memory, and previous work trip would surely be replayed in my mind. Things that were not significant at the time will surely be woven into an intricate plot that will emerge as clear as the light of day now that I could put it all into context. Like a detective attempting to crack an unsolved mystery, I would embark on a comprehensive search for all the evidence and leave no stone unturned. In that moment at the photo center, I knew that I would enter the investigatory phase soon. What I did not know is how much it would consume me and lead to some of the most impactful and devastating discoveries of my story.

Snap back to the Walmart photo center.

Christy seemed to be deeply focused on her task. She was methodically transferring photos from her phone, editing them, printing the photos and then diligently organizing them into different themes. As she did this, I meandered around the electronics section. Then the book section. Then the movies and music section. Then back to the electronics section.

I pretended to be interested in "3 for $20" DVD sales and the latest curved screen televisions. All the while, I kept my focus on her. Straining when I could to see if there were any photos in which she and Matt were together. I did not see any in my attempts, but I also did not see any of me and her either. These self-inflicted competitive mind games were just beginning, and they were not going to stop.

She finally took stock of her surroundings and I pretended like I was just getting back to meet her at the photo center.

"Hey there! How's it going?" I asked from an aisle away.

She replied, "Going well. I have got a few photos that are being a bit tricky, but I am almost done. Hey, would you mind picking up some cold medicine for me? I am not sure if it is allergies or if I have something coming on. I think it's over in the pharmacy section by the registers."

She then asked, "Do you mind if I finish up here then meet you to checkout?" Christy made a seemingly normal request and I needed to respond in kind.

Back to my performance.

"Sure thing! Do you want the powerful stuff or the non-drowsy?"

Like a good and dutiful husband, I went to the pharmacy section and picked up some Sudafed. I walked over to the checkout as Christy was just getting there. We exchanged some trivial pleasantries with the cashier and made our way out of the store. On the way out, I began to think about the agony of the drive to the store and how difficult the drive back would surely be. It was a total Godsend when her parents called her cell phone. The car we were driving did not have Bluetooth capabilities, so she took the call with the phone pressed against her ear and chatted away with her parents all the way back to Denver. I could only hear one half of the conversation and just stayed quiet for the entire ride. That was fine by me.

-6-

Hiding in Plain Sight

After the trip to Walmart, Christy and I did not have much time before we would have to head over to the neighborhood brewery to meet our friends for the afternoon's events. It was nearing one o'clock as I pulled into the alleyway behind our home and opened the garage door, so we only had about an hour to get ready and then head out the door again. As I was carefully maneuvering the car back into our assigned spot at the condo, Christy was still on the phone, chatting away with her parents. I shifted the car into park and grabbed a bag as I hopped out. Christy did the same and we both began to climb the stairs to the condo unit.

We were physically walking together but we were completely disconnected mentally. She was engrossed in her phone conversation. I was engrossed in the visualization and memorization of the damning text between Christy and Matt. I reviewed every word and emoticon in my mind. I sought to understand the contextual meaning behind every punctuation mark and parentheses. I was compartmentalizing and pretending adequately enough to cloak my feelings and thoughts. However, that did not mean I was completely shutting them out.

As we walked back into the house, Christy set her phone to mute and asked, "Hey, what time do we have to meet everybody?"

I said that we should probably leave in about forty-five minutes.

"Okay, well I still need to pack, so I'll start pulling stuff together now, but I'll probably need to do some more after we get home later." Christy's response was terse and matter of fact.

I felt her response was somewhat reflective of her feelings towards our plans that afternoon. Yes, they would be fun and enjoyable, but they were inconvenient for her. Especially if she were looking to thoughtfully pack all the items and outfits that she thought Matt would like best.

I am sure her current feelings of the inconvenience of our marriage was simply a continuation of a narrative that she had fed herself leading up to this weekend. It was a narrative that any participation in the "we" or "me" of our relationship was at a detriment to her own personal ambitions and desires. She was spending this afternoon with friends as a favor to me.

I wonder if she relied on this narrative heavily to internally provide a rationale for her betrayal. I wonder if it was part of the accumulation of events in which she felt she was giving to the relationship at her personal "detriment." Was this the justification she needed to maliciously rip me apart without me knowing? Who knows what she was actually thinking, but it is hard for me not to think of it that way.

I was trying to grasp at small victories that day. Getting through the trip to Walmart felt like a small victory. After we had arrived back from the errand, I pretty much just wasted time pacing around the house as Christy started her packing process. The minutes slowly ticked by and I held my tongue as she started laying out her clothes. In addition to her jeans, shorts and blouses were a pile of bathing suits, bras and panties. My mind raced as the scenarios started to well up in my mind about how and when Matt would be seeing those items for himself. I simply just turned on a music channel on the television and paced.

Finally, the time came to head over to the brewery. I let Christy know that it was just about time to get going and she took a break from backing to put on a coat and shoes. Getting out the door to go meet friends felt like I had cleared a massive hurdle. We walked over to the brewery together in relative silence. Again, this was not that different than much of our time together lately. In the months prior, this type of silence was uncomfortable and tense because I thought we were both on the same page of being too much in our own heads and simply not communicating well. Today, the silence was more than welcome. I was certainly in my own head, but I had no intention of disclosing anything if the question, "What's on your mind?" popped up.

Walking into that brewery was like a breath of fresh air. The friends we were meeting there were admittedly more friends of mine than they were of Christy's. However, this certainly was not for lack of effort by these friends or me to include Christy as a key member of the group.

This brewery is only a few blocks from the condo and holds a fitness social group on Tuesday nights. You know what, let me clarify further as that may sound more intimidating than it actually is. This is a group of friends that meet up after work on Tuesday nights, go for a short jog around a local park for about thirty minutes, then hang out for the next two to three hours enjoying discounted beer back at the brewery.

Christy and I had only started meeting up with this group a few months earlier. I quickly became an integral part of the group and met some of the best friends I will have in my life. Those are the same friends who we met up with on that Saturday and I will always be grateful for their friendship in that moment. Call it selfish, but I did feel like this group was mine. That is because I put in the effort to cultivate relationships within this group.

For several years since relocating to Denver, Christy and I had talked about making a concerted effort to "get out there" and meet some friends. We had been going to this local brewery for the better part of the year and would consistently see a flyer for this running group on the window near the entrance.

Christy would always nudge me and say, "We should go and check it out some time."

For nearly a year we had this same conversation around that flyer. Then finally, one Tuesday, I decided to take the bull by the horns. Christy seemed more than happy to let me scope it out and report back. After feeling extremely nervous about walking alone into a new group, I quickly realized that these people were fun, genuine, and welcoming. I could not wait to report back to Christy that I had found some amazing people and that I was so excited for Christy to meet them.

In the weeks and months that followed, Christy came to hang out with this group from time to time, but not with the regularity that I had established. When she did join in, she would always rave about the great time she had. But that was when she did join in the gatherings.

More times than not, I would head out for work on Tuesday mornings and right before I left, I would ask her "Hey, do you want to meet the group at the brewery tonight?"

"Yeah! Sounds great! We need to head over there around six, right?" she would respond enthusiastically. When Christy was not travelling, she worked from home, so she did not have the pressure of a commute weighing on commitments outside of work.

I was always excited when I heard this response at first. It felt like we had found something that was ours. Something that we could bond over. So, the first couple of times she bailed because she "had a rough day" or "was feeling tired," I did not think much of it. At first, I would always offer, in fact insist, on staying home with her. She would respond, "No. No. You should go. Don't worry about me."

As time went by, Christy would always commit to attending when we planned it out on Tuesday mornings. Then, like clockwork, she would bail out just minutes before we were supposed to leave. Like clockwork, I would offer not to go, and with the same frequency she would say, "No, please go. You get so much energy and happiness when you go. They are such a great group of people. It makes me so happy to see the energy they give you."

That statement, made on multiple occasions, seemed so benign in those moments. What I came to learn in the weeks after I discovered her affair, is that Christy was thrilled that I had made this group of friends. Although I did not know the depth of her affair on that Saturday, I came to learn that she found relief in the friendships I was forming. She had realized her feelings for Matt had surpassed her feelings for me and she was planning her exit strategy. She claims it made her feel good that I had developed a network around me, because she truly did care about me. I claim that is a load of bullshit.

By the time we arrived at the brewery, there was already a good crowd there. About ten people had already arrived and a few more filtered in soon after we showed up. There were endless smiles and laughs all around. Several of my friends were already on their second beer and were hitting their Saturday afternoon stride. They did not have a care in the world.

I ordered myself and Christy a beer, just like I normally would.

"I'll keep the tab open," I said to the bartender.

I was going to enjoy the next few hours. Again, my friends had no idea how much support they were providing for me on that Saturday afternoon.

As I mentioned earlier, the night before Christy and I had gone to see "Free Solo." Around this time, it was the talk of the town as it was the Hollywood award season and it had been nominated for several awards. It seemed like the entire group had recently seen it. Those two hours documenting the story of a man free climbing El Capitan in Yosemite provided great conversation fodder for this crew. This was an athletic and outdoorsy Colorado group. They just ate it up.

I lost myself in the conversation with them about the movie. Christy was sitting next to me, but I was hardly engaging with her. Occasionally, I would prod myself with a mental reminder to make a superficial attempt to bring her into the conversation. If someone made an observation that tangentially related to the experience Christy and I had when we had watched the movie, I would seize on the opportunity.

"I know, we were just saying that too!" I would ecstatically proclaim to both validate my friends' observation, as well as acknowledge that I was not completely ignoring Christy.

However, she seemed to be really enjoying the conversation as well. She seemed to be just as at ease as all my friends. She had apparently developed quite the skill to compartmentalize her life effectively.

About an hour passed by and the group decided to take the walk downtown to the area near the skating rink. It was still a warm day even as the sun was starting to get lower in the sky in the mid-afternoon of that February day. As we walked, the cool, crisp air started to creep its way in, but no one seemed to mind. The group was laughing, chatting and just having a great time! For so many it was just a carefree, boozy day with great friends. At least on a superficial level, I had allowed it to be the same for me as well.

Once we arrived at the skating rink, there was a brief snapback to my current reality. The rink may have been free, but the rental skates were not and the line to get them was substantial. The jovial members of the group temporarily disbanded to stake their respective places in line. Christy and I stood together in line in relative silence. It was not because we were not talking to each other, it is just that we did not have anything to talk about. I was happy to avoid any meaningful conversation with her and apparently, she felt the same.

Finally, we made it to the skate rental booth and procured our skates. As we went back to lace them up, a thought crossed my mind. Matt had played ice hockey all his life and was quite good at the sport. In fact, Christy and I had gone with some of her co-workers to watch one of his amateur league playoff games a few years back, before we moved to Colorado.

A wave of insecurity seemed to briefly wash over me. I am an athletic person with above average balance and hand-eye coordination, but I had only been ice skating a handful of times in my life.

"I bet you she is getting a kick out of the fact that Matt is better than me at this," I thought to myself.

These waves of competitiveness kept creeping in and would be a consistent theme over the following days and weeks. As we were putting on our skates, Christy seemed to struggle with the tightness of her pair. She did not know if they were too tight or not tight enough.

"I bet you wish your boyfriend was here to help you," I thought to myself. "I'm sure Matt would know exactly how to lace up your skates perfectly."

We made our way onto the ice. I will not say it came back to me quickly, but after a few instances of instinctual panic when I felt my skate slip from underneath me, I started to build up enough confidence to jump into the counterclockwise whirlpool of people. It was a small rink that was packed with everyone from toddlers to hockey "has-beens" trying to reclaim their glory days. It was the kind of chaos that did not really allow for people to skate together. Your most sure way to get around the rink was to find a gap and go for it. Every person for themselves.

We skated for about an hour before the group seemed to have had enough. We all congregated near a corner of the rink and asked a generous passerby if he would take a picture of us. Ordinarily, I would make sure to find Christy and be next to her for these types of pictures. However, on this occasion, I was more than happy to envelope myself in the middle of my friends. Christy stood on the edge of the picture. I still have that picture and look back at it from time to time. It reminds me that I made the effort to build a community around Christy and me. Meanwhile, Christy put just enough effort in to simply stand at the edge. This must have allowed her to step out of our marriage and into her other life with relative ease.

After the picture, the group made its way over to a local restaurant for some pizza and beer. At this point the sun had disappeared and the invasion of cold air provided a stark reminder that it was still February, so we quickly hurried to get to the warmth of the restaurant. As we entered, Christy let me know that she needed to get home soon to finish up her packing. We agreed to have one more drink with the group and then head home in an Uber.

-7-

Do Not Even Think About Touching Me

As much as the afternoon and evening's activities with friends provided some temporary relief, climbing into the Uber to head back to the condo immediately brought reality back into focus. After we settled into the Honda Accord to start our five-minute ride back to the condo, Christy asked if I had a good time with my friends.

"Yeah, it was great to see everybody. They are such a good crew," I responded.

Christy acknowledged my response with a similar sentiment.

"They are such a fun group. I am so glad you found them. I feel like we are really building our community here!"

Our community! Did she really just say that? During this phase where I knew about her affair, but she was not aware that I knew about her deceit, it seemed like I could not help but internally roll my eyes every time I heard a statement like that. Christy continued to chat about what she needed to do once we arrived home. She obviously had to pack, but she also had to pull some meeting materials together. She stated that she would probably be up late trying to take care of everything. She then brought up the topic of transportation to the airport the next morning.

"I can just take an Uber to the airport in the morning. I will probably need to leave around six. I will also probably hit the ground running pretty hard when I get to Florida and probably will not have much time eat when I get there, so I would like to get to DIA with plenty of time to make sure I can grab breakfast before my flight."

As she laid out her transportation plans, a peculiar feeling came over me. I knew, at least on a symbolic level, that tomorrow would be the last time I would ever see her in the phase of life that we had been living in up until now. Even though I had discovered the truth about her betrayal, we were still operating "normally" on the path of life that had been in motion since we were teenagers. But I knew that all this work trip did was buy me time for the inevitable. Life as we knew it was ending the next day.

This realization hit me like a ton of bricks.

I blurted out, "Hey, I can give you a ride to the airport in the morning."

She responded that I did not have to, but I insisted.

"Okay, if you do not mind giving me a ride, that would be great!" As Christy accepted my offer to drive to the airport in the morning, our Uber pulled up in front of the condo. As we walked up to the front door, I primarily focused on finishing off the trip on the application. Five stars and a three-dollar tip.

At this point it was closing in on nine o'clock at night. I would have to be up around five-thirty in the morning to get dressed, brew the coffee for the ride and head out the door. When we entered the condo, Christy immediately headed into the bedroom to continue her packing process. I needed something mindless to pass the time separately.

I grabbed a beer from the refrigerator, kicked my shoes off and started skimming through Netflix. As usually happens, I flipped through a series of trailers for new shows but eventually settled on some time with Steve Carrell and "The Office." I started with an episode called "The Duel." It is the one where Andy finds out that Angela is having an affair with Dwight. It is a hilarious episode (Honestly, aren't all the episodes of "The Office" hilarious?) and I could not help but have it play on the television. Christy was packing for her romantic rendezvous with Matt while I was watching this particular episode. I will never know for sure, but I really hope she could at least sense the irony.

I laid on the couch for a while as Christy continued to pack. The repartee between Jim, Pam, Michael and Dwight certainly provided some much-needed superficial levity. However, I certainly was feeling the weight and gravity of what was before me pressing harder and harder on my chest.

I had lived a lifetime in that one day. Earlier that morning, I woke up a married man who was concerned about Christy's recent suspicious behavior. I then found the devastating text messages she received from Matt and immediately navigated a way just to make it through the day. Now, I had successfully navigated through the day and felt like I had just arrived right back to where I had started.

Around eleven o'clock I decided to head to bed. Christy was still organizing items for her meeting, now in the spare room of the condo. After the normal routine of dental hygiene, I proclaimed from the hallway, "Hey Christy, hope the prep is going well. I am going to head to bed, and I'll set my alarm for five-thirty. Love you."

Why did I say those last two words? Was it simply out of habit? They seemed to just slip out. It is amazing how I was becoming hyper analytical of every behavior that just twenty-four hours earlier was commonplace and mindless.

She responded, "Be there in a bit. Love you too."

The thing is, there is a falsehood that is perpetuated to and by all starry eyed, young couples out there. The notion that all two people need for their fairytale relationship is to love each other with all their heart and that is all they will ever need. The world be damned.

I think that is also why it is so easy for many people to see an affair as a "black and white" offence in which it is easy for the betrayed partner to simply dismiss the cheating partner because they betrayed this fairytale love. For me, I certainly did not love

Christy at that moment. At least not in the traditional romantic sense. However, what I did love was the normalcy that an investment in a life with Christy had created. It is easy to shut off love for the individual after this type of betrayal, but it is extremely difficult to shut off the love of a past, present and future that you have created with her.

I set the alarm on my phone and crawled into bed. I faced away from the door and closed my eyes, but I could not sleep. It was the first time since my run earlier in the day that I had been alone with my thoughts and my mind was racing. I still had some sort of illusion in my mind that maybe, just maybe, her physical romantic relationship with Matt had not started yet and I could still stop it if I disclosed what I knew and demanded she not go on her trip. Maybe there was a chance that I could stop this.

On the other hand, it was a certainty that if she did go on the trip, their relationship would be both emotionally and physically complete. Thoughts were swirling around my head faster than I could comprehend them. As soon as I could hone in on one thought, another would pop up with seemingly paramount importance. I laid there awake, drowning in my own thoughts.

About forty-five minutes after I went to bed, I could hear Christy sealing off the last of her luggage and starting her bedtime routine. There was something disgusting to me about the notion that she was about to climb into the same bed as me. I knew I could not ask her to sleep elsewhere, or even go sleep in the spare room myself. That would surely raise suspicion that I was upset and possibly on to her schemes.

I laid there as still as I possibly could. I had situated myself such that my back was facing the entrance to the bedroom as I faced the far wall and window. I kept my eyes open and just stared ahead as I felt the shift in the bedding as she laid down.

I immediately thought to myself, "Breathe like you are sleeping!" I then concentrated all my energy on taking slow, deep breaths indicative of how one breathes while asleep. Obviously, I had never heard what my own breathing sounded like when I sleep, so I primarily was basing this exercise on replicating what I had heard from others.

She quietly settled in, nestling her head into the pillow as her body relaxed while the cold temperatures of the previously dormant blanket and sheets gave way to the effect of her body heat. As I laid there, waiting anxiously for her to be still and fall asleep, I started thinking to myself, "Do not even think about touching me!"

I am not exactly sure why that was such a concern for me. I mean, Christy and I had not been together in any type of passionate way for quite some time and if we were, it was generally sporadic and more out of habit than the result of a burning desire.

The overwhelming odds were that she was not going to try and initiate anything tonight. However, for some reason I was terrified that I would not know how to react if she did. I was honestly repulsed by the idea. The mere thought of her so much as trying to hold my hand, putting her hand on my back or even kissing my head goodnight were making my chest pound and my body clench.

That phrase, "Do not even think about touching me!" played repeatedly in my head.

This may sound ridiculous to most men, and maybe even some women, but I genuinely thought that any attempt of Christy to initiate anything with me that night would take me to a new low. I already felt rejected. I could not handle the thought of also being used. I also could not handle the thought of being in a position to turn her away, because then I would probably be just feeding even more into her excitement to fall into Matt's arms the next night. So that same thought just kept on going in my mind.

"Do not even think about fucking touching me!"

Although I was pretending to be asleep by lying completely still and controlling my breathing, I was extremely alert. The room was noticeably dark. The moon was beginning its new phase, so the typical ambient glow of the night sky was non-existent that night. Since the darkness masked one of my senses, the others seemed to be heightened.

Every time Christy shifted; I could feel it. I could hear every breath she took. I do not know if she was uncomfortable, nervous or possibly excited for her trip, but she never seemed to settle in that night. I kept waiting for a stillness. I kept waiting for her breath to reach a slow and consistent cadence. I kept waiting, but it did not happen. I laid there awake, all night. Little did I know at the time that this sleepless night was only the first of many to come.

The seconds stretched into minutes. The minutes crawled their way to hours. Finally, around five o'clock on Sunday morning, Christy's alarm sounded. She did not waste any time. She leapt out of bed and immediately got to work on preparing herself for her day of travel. I heard the bathroom door close and the initiation of the whirling sound of the fan. A soft glow cut through the darkness from the sliver of light escaping from the bottom of the bathroom door. I took that few minutes to finally relax. I even fell asleep for about fifteen minutes. Although short lived, it was marvelous. The physical need to sleep momentarily won the battle against my restless mind.

My alarm went off at five-thirty and it shook me awake with such a force. A panic immediately gripped me as I incoherently struggled to quickly gather my thoughts and figure out where I was. The thought even drifted through my mind that everything had been a hellish nightmare. But I quickly got my bearings and took stock of my surroundings. Reality set back in. Sleeping was the respite. Reality was my hellish nightmare.

I slowly shuffled to the second bathroom and turned on the shower. I stood there with my hand against the wall as the hot water cascaded onto my head and down my back. I was not actively crying, but my eyes were perpetually coated with tears, mixed in with the shower water that dripped down from my hair. The restlessness of the previous night dyed the whites of my eyes a rosy pink.

I had made it past the first day. I took pride in that. I had achieved my goal to make it one day. But nothing prepared me for the fact that the subsequent days would not be any easier. Each one would bring different emotions, reactions and actions. At least on the first day, I was rested. I would have to navigate these subsequent days without energy, without an appetite and without sleep.

I had made it through day one. On to day two.

-8-

Leaving on a Jet Plane

I could have never predicted the loneliness that was awaiting me that morning. After I finished my shower and started getting dressed, I returned to the compartmentalizing mindset that had served me well the day before in an effort to continue acting normally. As I brewed the morning coffee, Christy was frantically maneuvering around the condo to check and recheck her luggage and carry-on baggage. We had about ten minutes before we had to leave for the airport to be on time. There was nothing I could really do to help her pack, so I just sat on the couch as the coffee machine dripped away while she scurried about.

Then there was a task that I would apparently be useful for. "Hey Sean, can you please help me for a second?" Christy exclaimed.

I walked into the room where Christy had been packing. You would think a bomb had gone off in the room as most of her clothes were strewn across the bed, dresser and floor. She tended to pack like this. It is almost like the strategy was to start with everything in the closet and then narrow those items down to the select pieces that made the cut. Just as usual, she had packed but was leaving a mess of her clothes in her wake.

She stated, "Sorry, I'll clean this up when I get back next weekend. I just do not have time to do it now." This was her routine.

Then she handed me a luggage scale and asked me to weigh her luggage. I looped the hook of the scale around the main baggage handle and pulled it off the floor. Fifty-three pounds.

"Shit!" Christy exclaimed.

She gave me this look of frustration as if I had summoned an extra three pounds to magically appear in her bag, putting her over the airline weight limit of fifty pounds.

"I don't have time for this!" she said with exasperation.

Besides the logistical coordination of walking out the door of the condo, that was the last exchange I had with Christy as a married couple in our home. I did not know it would be at that moment, but as the week would progress, revelations of the nature of her affair would come to light. By the time I saw her again, I no longer would consider myself married to her.

It is a strange feeling to know that everything you do; it will be for the last time. Everything that seemed so mundane and routine before, were now events in which every detail seemed to be highlighted by a spotlight. Closing the condo door behind me. Turning the key to lock the door. Lugging the bags to the elevator. Feeling the slight shudder of the elevator as it came to a stop in the garage. Loading up the car. Settling in for the drive to drop Christy at the airport. I had done these exact tasks countless times in our marriage. Yet today, the finality of her betrayal brought them into focus. We would never be the same.

Survival was still the name of the game. I was still in performance mode. I knew I would be entering a new phase today when Christy left. This phase seemed like it should be easier to navigate. Christy would be on her trip and I would have time to myself to craft my strategy to confront her about what I knew. I wanted to make sure my strategy was comprehensive and could not just be discarded as paranoia or a stupid misunderstanding.

From the little I had been able to research the day before, a very common reaction when confronted about an affair is for the betraying spouse to vehemently deny it and try to flip it into an unfair accusation by the betrayed spouse.

In my case, Christy may respond with something like, "Are you serious? What, you do not trust me, so you have to go behind my back? You are willing to destroy our whole marriage because of a few joke texts? That is extremely hurtful, and I cannot believe you would do something like that!"

In reality, I only had those two text messages and I was already having doubts creeping in about what they actually meant. Maybe they were just a joke? Maybe she wanted me to find them to force us into a difficult conversation that would help our relationship? If so, maybe Matt was just acting to help her? I mean, he is a mutual friend.

I know those thoughts and doubts about the nature of the text messages sound ridiculous to a person of rational mind. As I sit here writing this, thinking back on those thoughts, they were ridiculous rationalizations to have. But you must understand, when you marry someone and have built an entire life with them, you are conditioned to give them every benefit of the doubt. As irrational as it may have been, my life and well-being were completely interwoven in Christy's life. I think back on it now and believe that the irrational benefit of the doubt is a product of your own survival instincts. It was not about whether Christy and Matt actually did the things that the text messages insinuated (rather explicitly stated), but it was the impacts those actions would have on my life.

As we rounded the on ramp to Interstate 70 to head eastbound for the airport, these thoughts were crossing my mind. As I quietly drove, I started thinking about how I would use that week to build my case. I wanted to make sure that any denial or counteraccusation she threw at me would be proven baseless by my preparation and knowledge.

For now though, I had to successfully drive to the airport and get Christy there in time for her flight. It would take us about twenty-five minutes to get there. In about twenty-five minutes I will have successfully pulled the wool over her eyes enough to avoid prematurely disclosing what I knew. I decided to strike up a conversation to get her talking. I had recently taken a marketing course on asking open-ended questions for work. I tried to use the skills I had learned there to have a twenty-five minute conversation with my own wife.

"How are you feeling about the meetings?" I asked Christy.

It was obviously the main thing on her mind. She had been either talking about how nervous she was about the delivery of her material or how excited she was to see her colleagues for a few weeks prior. Little did I know, she was particularly excited to see one colleague in particular, Matt. I really began to wonder how they were even pulling off their affair.

Up until about a year prior, Christy had reported directly to Matt. Matt even approved Christy's transfer to Denver when we decided to move to Colorado in 2016. How many raises, promotions, and bonuses were based on their relationship? How many of her numerous trips back to the headquarter office in New Jersey were actually necessary? She was traveling back and forth on the company dime for nearly three years at a cadence of about once a month. About a year prior, Matt was promoted to the Director of Human Resources (which is incredibly ironic) and one of Christy's colleagues, Dan, was promoted to take Matt's role. Dan had been Christy's direct supervisor for about a year at this point. How did he not know about an affair? Were Christy and Matt really that skilled at leading double lives? Apparently so.

Christy talked nearly the whole drive to the airport. She explained that most of her team was arriving in Florida on a flight from Newark about two hours before she would arrive. Her plan was to land in Fort Lauderdale, rent a car and head to the resort where the meeting was being hosted, which was about thirty minutes from the airport.

Even though I was aware of the nature of the meeting, she

described it in detail again in the car. It was a retreat of sorts for the company's executive leaders, department heads and rank and file management personnel. It was one of those corporate style retreats where the intention is to transport the decision makers from their day to day routine to a cocoon of lavishness and free thought. It was a chance for managers from all over the country to connect, build personal relationships and exchange ideas for the betterment of the business.

Being in human resources, particularly in her specific department of human resources, Christy's role was to facilitate gatherings which would strategically foster conversation and free flow of insights and ideas. Her team had come up with the "living room" theme, a cozy space to create an environment similar to sitting around your home with friends and family. By doing this, the team hoped to build a comfort level amongst the managers to drop their professional filters and speak their minds in an environment with limited judgment or consequences.

About twenty minutes into the drive down I-70, I began my methodical drifting from the through travel lanes to the exit lanes for Pena Boulevard. As we exited onto Pena, we were only about ten minutes away from the "Departures" ramp. Christy was continuing to talk about her upcoming meeting and then brought up Matt as a topic of conversation.

"I'm a little nervous about making sure this all goes well, but I can only imagine the stress Matt is feeling," she stated.

In Matt's position as Director of Human Resources, he was not only in charge of leading the team to facilitate all the retreat meetings, but he was also an executive level participant as well.

"He has been working so hard and I know he has been stressing about this." She continued. "I just hope he gets a chance to take a break and relax after the meetings are done. He certainly deserves it."

I cannot believe she could be so bold in her statements right in front of me. I had discovered their text messages the day before and had put two and two together that her request to spend a couple extra days at the beach was very likely a romantic getaway for them to have unencumbered time for their passionate love affair. Here she was, literally stating to me how she just hopes that Matt can relax after this stressful time, while fully knowing that she was going behind my back to help him "relax." The mere thought of the image of Christy helping Matt to "relax" nearly made me sick.

I choked back my visceral disdain for the words that were spewing from her toxic mouth. I choked out the only response that I felt was appropriate.

I responded, "Sounds stressful. I hope he gets through the next few days and is able to spend some quality time with Leslie and the kids. With him working so hard, I hope he can find the balance to also have time for his marriage and his children. I know I always missed my dad when he had to go on business trips, and I was always so excited when he came home!"

My response had to at least nick the surface of her conscience. It had to broaden the potential impact of her deception beyond the narrow scope of my feelings and shed light on how her actions would devastate a beautiful family. Leslie was a loyal and loving wife to Matt. His kids adored him. As far as his kids knew, Leslie and Matt's marriage was the pillar of truth and goodness in their life. I hoped she would at least feel a little tinge of remorse.

Instead, she responded. "I agree. I hope he and Leslie get to spend some quality time with the kids, as well. They are such a great family and he is such a good dad."

Her response brought back to light that I could not simply avoid the reality before me. Christy's deception had become so commonplace in her mind. She thought she had everyone fooled. As we pulled up to the curbside drop off, I took in the last minutes of playing along with her deception. Every detail of those last moments with the woman I called my wife remains crystal clear.

The soft pink hue of first light on the mountains. The orange and pink glow to the east before the sun rose which softly transitioned to a harsh navy blue of nighttime still lingering over the west.

I will always remember lifting her bags out of the back of our car as I had done numerous times before. I placed her luggage up on the curb. Then I proceeded to carefully place her laptop backpack on top of the larger piece of carry-on luggage.

I turned around and gave Christy a hug. She pulled her head back and gave me a kiss.

"Have a safe flight." I politely stated.

She responded. "Thanks, I love you."

I could not bring myself to say that word this morning, so instead I responded. "You too, talk to you soon."

With that, Christy gathered the baggage on the curb as I climbed back into the driver's seat of the car. I waited as I watched her walk through the automatic doors. Door 608 at Denver International Airport. 6:27 AM. February 3, 2019. The exact place and moment my ex-wife walked through those airport doors. For me, it marked the moment in which our marriage, at least the one we had been living in, was over.

I remained watching as the outline of her body was slowly silhouetted by the tinted airport windows until it consumed her completely. She was now gone. I had not told anyone and now I was alone. Completely and devastatingly alone.

-9-

Completely Alone

I shifted the car to "drive" and carefully pulled away from the departure area of the airport. Being a Sunday morning, Super Sunday no less, the airport was profoundly quiet. Typically, DIA is bustling with people, even at odd hours. But today, I could count on one hand the number of vehicles with me up on the departures ramp. This was a good thing as all of the emotions that I had put in check for the last twenty-four hours seemed to well up at hit me all at once as soon as Christy walked through the airport doors.

My eyes were glassing over, and tears started filling my eyes as I drove away. The road was a blurry, gray mass in front of me. The white, dashed lane lines were barely distinguishable in my eyes. I was relying heavily on my previous knowledge of the road. I knew the curves and the quirks of Pena Boulevard. I knew the lane drops and the exit only merge points. This knowledge through experience was a key component of my ability to keep my vehicle on the pavement during that stretch. My mind was elsewhere. It was like that feeling of driving to a destination where you have been on such a version of autopilot that you cannot recall the details of how you arrived at your destination. This was similar, except along the way I know I was not seeing the road clearly because my vision was incredibly blurry, and my cognition was on everything but the road.

It is hard to really describe the profound nature of my emotional state as I drove away from the airport. The marriage I had to Christy was over. However, I was still married to her. I know many people see it as a very binary thing, you are either married or you are not married.

Drilling down further, the expectation is that a faithful spouse is a requirement for marriage and any breach of that means the marriage is over. It is amazing how quickly you discover that it really does not work that way. I mean, some people may react with much more of an immediate reaction than I did. But I am fairly certain that very few people have the mental, emotional and physical ability to just sever ties in an instant. Very few have the ability to just walk away from everything that was stable and secure in their marriage and their life in the instant before they discovered an affair. It is pure survival. The end of your marriage is also the end of your life as you know it. You cannot just simply say, "Oh well, there's half my life for nothing."

It is that survival instinct and indecision about what her affair meant for my life that was a debilitating burden on that drive back to Denver from the airport. Out of self-preservation, I could not give up any control of the situation to anybody. This was my life.

I was instantaneously filled with the need to curb any outside opinions that may influence the decisions that I had to make for my life. I felt that any person I told about what I had found would be a person that I would then have to explain my subsequent actions to. What if I decided to stay with Christy? How would any person I had told have any respect for me? Any person that I had told would surely hate Christy and what she did to me. How could that not affect my decision?

At the end of the day it is a very binary decision. Do I stay married to a cheater or do I divorce her for what she has done? In its basic essence, it is a simple decision. However, the logic and process to come to that decision is far more complex than many people care to think about. I think it is one of the cruelest impacts a cheating spouse has on their partner. Up until the moment I found out, I always thought that a cheating spouse deserves to be divorced and shamed for their actions. Friends and loved ones would agree and rally behind that decision. It is a simple black and white "non-starter" for sure, and it is actually a really easy way to justify divorce.

However, on that drive back from the airport, all I could think about was how I would preserve Christy's integrity, at least until I could figure out what I wanted. I did not want my life as I knew it to be over. I did not want Christy to have done the things she did, but I was compelled to put my marriage to my cheating wife above my need for short term support from my loved ones. This was all in the attempt to preserve my ability to make the biggest decision of my life without the influence of anybody else.

When I had this realization that I could not confide in anybody about what had happened and, at the same time, I had not yet told Christy what I knew, it left me in a tremendous state of limbo. During that drive back to Denver, I felt as if I had no one on the entire planet who knew me and what I was dealing with. I had never felt that level of loneliness before. It is an overwhelming sense of loneliness. The space between fear, sadness, guilt and indecision is a very dark place to be stuck. As someone who loves life and is an unabashed optimist, it pains me to say that I really did not care about living at that moment. The loneliness that surrounded me had made me numb to life. It dulled every sense. I felt no direction and no purpose for my life.

As I drove along I-70 westbound, this feeling made me cry so hard that it was debilitating. It was uncontrollable. It was the type of crying that you cannot hide. It was audible. It was raw. It was ugly. My grip on the wheel was extremely weak. I felt as if my body was completely limp. I was slouched in the driver seat, going through the motions of driving back home.

"Home?" I thought. "What home?"

Everything I had in my life at that point was directly tied to a decision I had made with Christy. I had nowhere to escape that I could call my own.

I was in the right lane, driving well under the speed limit. I was not in a rush to get anywhere. I really did not even know where I was going to go. Out of habit, I was driving towards the direction of the condo, but there was no structure to my actions. There was no destination. I was in such a trance that I did not realize I had started to drift right. I do not know for sure, but I could not have been more than a few inches from sideswiping the concrete barrier that frames the elevated viaduct north of downtown. The only thing that kept me from scraping across that barrier at fifty miles per hour was the taper of the barrier that occurs just before the Brighton Boulevard exit.

I had avoided a disaster. However, the fortunate taper of the barrier ultimately led to a bigger problem. I had drifted enough that I was heading straight into the barrier termination that separates the main highway from the exit ramp. I believe in God and I have had several unexplainable occurrences in my life which have reinforced my belief. I likened His intervention to disrupt my impending disastrous and likely fatal crash to the feeling where you are a little tired behind the wheel and something shakes you awake. Right before the point of no return, I was startled by a voice.

"Sean. Snap out of it!" I jerked the car left.

I did not miss the steel termination which was framed into the solid concrete barrier by much. It scared the shit out of me. Thinking back on how close my life came to ending on that car ride back from the airport is a stark reminder of how a life, even a normally vibrant and optimistic life, is no match for the devastating effects of a perceived loss of purpose. It is a purely evil feeling and in just that split second, it almost caused the end of me.

I needed purpose. As trivial as it was, I needed some plan of action to fill my time, and more importantly, my mind. Being that it was Super Sunday, I remember that one of my friends from the fitness group had invited Christy and me to a watch party at his house. Several my running group friends who I had just seen the day before would be there. I could not tell them anything, but I realized I desperately needed to be around friends. I could not make it through this day alone. The host of the party thought it would be fun if we incorporated a chili cook off into the event, thus providing entertainment, but more importantly, delicious and hot chili on that cold Sunday in February.

"I'll make my pork green chili," I thought to myself.

My task was defined. My purpose in life had become to stop by the grocery store and make a pot of green chili. It sounds pathetic and it was, but my life was at rock bottom and that green chili is what was going to keep me going.

I wish I could say that this was an isolated incident of trying to find purpose after that day. Unfortunately, it became a theme for my life that I still struggle with to this day. Luckily, the intensity of these experiences has lessened with time. But they are a reality of my experience now. Little did I know this at the time of my near accident, but in the minutes before I barely missed that barrier, I was experiencing a panic attack. A bout with severe anxiety from which my mind could not escape. I believe God intervened to provide immediate help during that first one. However, these attacks would be something I would have to learn to identify and overcome in the coming days and weeks. These attacks still plague me to this day, I have just acquired the skills to deal with them through experience.

The main thing I did learn that day is the way to overcome severe feelings of helplessness is to find purpose in something. Anything. On that Super Sunday, mine became how I would blow my friends away with my green chili recipe. I had made this chili several times and even people who do not really like spicy food seemed to enjoy it. I have even seen some family members who were hesitant to eat it at first, gleefully reheat it the next morning to smother it all over their scrambled eggs. I have brought it to office chili competitions and have won the top prize. So, to summarize, it is not bad.

As I continued my drive down I-70, I began to make a mental list of the ingredients I would need and what I already had at the condo. I needed a four-pound pork shoulder, Anaheim Chilies, chicken stock and tomatillos. So, I needed to stop in at a grocery store. The King Soopers grocery store was on my way. It was a relatively new grocery store in the ballpark neighborhood of Denver. This neighborhood where the grocery store is located is full of twenty-something transplants who are far more interested in sleeping off a hangover on a Sunday morning than beating the crowds to the grocery store at seven in the morning, so I expected that the store would be pretty empty. I took the exit for I-25 south, then Park Avenue. I had my first destination to fulfill my day's purpose.

I only needed four items. However, I was in such a daze that I meandered around the store for over an hour. Again, it took me over an hour to procure four items. This was because shopping at the grocery store was the activity my body was executing, but my mind was elsewhere. It must have been the fifth or sixth time I walked past the chicken stock in the soup aisle before I finally saw it and plucked it off the shelf. I was completely preoccupied the few times I walked down that aisle. The loneliness was quickly becoming way too much to handle. I began to think that I would not make it another day without letting someone in.

I started scouring my mental rolodex. I knew I could not tell anyone in my family, at least not yet. Not only would it be extremely difficult to separate my decision making process from the outrage that family members would obviously have towards Christy, but I also knew there was a very real possibility that this information would leak to other family members and loved ones over the coming days and weeks. The same thing went for mutual friends. I did not know what the outcome of any of this would be, but I was scared to death of what the post-affair world would look like if I would ultimately have to choose between severing friendships and reconciling with Christy. I could control my ability to forgive and reconcile, but I could not say the same for friends and family.

I also could not ask them to fake the way they felt about her either. I was scared that a disclosure of this magnitude to a person in which Christy and I had a mutual relationship may ultimately lead to a choice between my relationship with Christy and my relationship with everyone else I cared about. Irrational or not, that is the way I felt in that grocery store.

So, no mutual friends and no family. I started thinking about people that I had enough of a close relationship with to not only disclose this information, but also trust their discretion. I needed to confide in someone who did not have a relationship with Christy in any greater capacity than they knew of her because she was my wife.

"My running club," I thought to myself.

There were a few people in the group that Christy had developed a superficial relationship with so I carefully thought about who would be best to speak with. After a few minutes of thinking about it, I decided I would really like a woman's perspective on what I believed Christy was doing. I decided that I would reach out to Monica. She had unknowingly helped me the previous day by quickly revising the logistics of the ice-skating event. Today, I would be asking her to knowingly help me understand and navigate the hell that my life had become.

-10-

I Have to Tell Someone

The drive from the airport and meandering around the grocery store will truly stay with me as the loneliest I have ever felt in my life. There is a common saying that something is so bad that, "I would not wish this on my worst enemy." I have heard it many times in stories of war and death but had never felt it for myself before. I honestly remember thinking that I had such a selfless love and care of Christy that I would not wish any of what she was putting me through, on her. I truly do not think I would have lasted the day without the ability to reach out to somebody. I HAD to let somebody in.

As I stood in the checkout line at the grocery store, I typed out a text message to Monica.

"Hey, are you around later this morning or early this afternoon? Had something come up and really need to talk to someone about it."

I hit send and tried to put it out of my mind. I had learned my lesson yesterday during my run about the severe manic nature brought on by simply staring at my phone and waiting for a response. I put the phone in my pocket and resolved that I would not look at it until I exited the grocery store.

I waited patiently as the goods of the customer in front of me slowly moved down the conveyor belt towards the scanner. He kindly reached over his items and placed the rubber separator down on the conveyor belt. A polite gesture to signify that I was welcome to start placing my items on the belt behind his items. It may sound simple and overstated, but those simple and kind aspects of humanity were not lost on me that day. I craved them and latched on to them. I cherished them in a way I felt like I had not before.

As the seemingly congenial patron in front of me completed his transaction on the automated pin pad, my phone vibrated in my pocket. I placed my hand on it through the outside of my jeans, but then stopped. I told myself I would not look at it until I was outside of the grocery store. I patiently waited for the clerk to start scanning my items. It vibrated again. A few seconds went by. Then again.

It seemed maddening that I had given myself this trivial mental exercise to avoid looking at my phone for a matter of five minutes while I checked out of the grocery store. Surely one of those alerts had to be a text from Monica responding to my digital plea. But I used this as a simple test of my psychological ability. I need to focus on the task at hand. My pork shoulder, chicken stock, Anaheim peppers and tomatillos slid toward the scanner.

"Good morning!" the cheerful clerk exclaimed. "How's your day going so far?"

Her question was in keeping with social custom. It was more of a pleasantry and not a genuine inquisition of how my day was actually going so far.

Could you imagine if I had responded, "Well, I just dropped my wife off at the airport after I found out yesterday that she has been cheating on me. I cried all the way here and almost slammed head-on into a concrete barrier on I-70 because I was so distraught. So now I am here at the grocery store, collecting items to make a chili that is literally the sole purpose of my life today."

I imagine a stranger did not want to really know how my day was, so I answered with the customary, "Not too bad, how is yours going?"

I faked a minute or two of pleasantries as I completed the

transaction. My items conveniently fit in one bag. I quickly snatched it off the bulkhead at the end of the checkout terminal and hurried toward the door. The automatic doors slid apart and the cool February air rushed around me. I quickly reached into my pocket. I had three messages. Two of them were from Monica. One was from Christy.

I checked Monica's messages first. Call it selfish, but I needed to focus on what I needed first. Christy could wait.

"Hey Sean, yeah I can chat!" The affirmative first message from Monica hit me like a warm breeze on that cold morning. I was not completely alone.

The second message went on to say, "I'm running a 5K in Wash Park this morning, but am happy to meet up after, probably around 11 if that works for you?"

I then checked Christy's message. "Boarded my flight. Love you."

Christy's words felt so logistical, cold and disingenuous compared to Monica's messages. I had more trust in the genuineness of a friend than I did in the statement of "Love you" from my wife. I shifted back to Monica's message, feeling the need to lock in a plan. I needed my next objective for the day.

"Oh cool, I did not realize there was a race this morning! 11 is perfect. Just hoping to chat about something for a bit. Want to grab a coffee?"

I then suggested we meet at a little boutique coffee shop and cafe near Wash Park.

"Sounds good! See you there," Monica responded.

Success! I had my plan that would help me get through the morning.

My response to Monica's messages was genuine. By contrast, my response to Christy's message would be emotionless and robotic.

"Great," I responded back to Christy.

That is all I could muster for a response. I felt it was all she deserved. I decided to dial back my role as Christy's husband to logistical only. I needed to use all the remaining capacity in my emotional tank for myself.

I wanted to get some exercise that day, even though it was just about the last thing I had energy for. I had barely eaten the night before and had no appetite for breakfast on that Sunday morning. I decided that I would run to the coffee shop to meet Monica later that morning and then would run home afterwards. This would likely have me arriving back at my home about an hour or so before I would have to head over to the party with my chili. I now needed to get home quickly and start the cooking process, so it had time to simmer for a few hours. All the sudden, my day was busy, but it was exactly what I needed. I hurried to my car and started the rest of my journey home.

Upon arriving home, I did not even bother to put the groceries in the refrigerator. Within five minutes of walking in the door I was browning pork chunks covered in salt and cumin. I had the oven preheating and ready to roast the Anaheim peppers. There were onions, garlic and tomatillos to chop. My movements were a repetitive dance between a cutting board and an Instant Pot. Within a half hour, I had all the ingredients in the pot and the lid secure. I set it to cook the chili over the next few hours.

It was a hurried process. I needed to get the chili going and get out the door. The run to the coffee shop would take me about twenty-five minutes and it was almost ten-thirty. I had agreed to meet Monica at eleven and I did not want to be rude and late. She was taking time out of her day to talk to a friend about God knows what. The last thing I would want would be for her to be sitting at the cafe, waiting for me and wondering if I would show up. With my athletic gear on and my shoes laced up, I set off.

My run to the coffee shop felt clunky and disjointed. It was in stark contrast to my run around Wash Park right after I checked

Christy's phone just a day earlier. Yesterday, I was fueled by adrenaline and deep, calculating thought to pass the time. Not to mention, it was after a full night of sleep and a nice, healthy dinner the night prior. But today's run was hampered by fatigue from a sleepless night, emotional distress and an empty stomach. The notion of telling Monica was also starting to weigh on me. I was becoming increasingly conflicted about letting somebody in on my story. What if Monica judges that I kept what I knew from Christy? What if she tells somebody what I told her? What if she disagrees with my conclusion that Christy is having an affair, or worse, what if she simply just thinks I am overreacting, and I wasted her time?

After a huffing and puffing struggle to get to the coffee shop, I scanned the outdoor seating area to see if Monica was already there. It was a cool, but sunny Denver day. There were plenty of people sipping coffees with dogs leased to their chairs. Those in the sun were donning slick sunglasses and tee shirts. Those who were sitting in the shade were shivering under layers of Patagonia fleece. Typical Colorado, where there is a twenty-degree difference between sunshine and shade. She was not sitting outside, so I made my way into the cafe.

The cafe is small with a lot of tightly spaced tables. It is built out of an old house, so it had a very cozy feel to it. I realized Monica had not arrived yet, so I joined the line to order a coffee. This place was definitely too hipster for me, but I hung in there. I kept scanning the chalk scrapings on the blackboard to figure out what a regular coffee cost. Based on the multi-colored chalk writing, they had every imaginable hot beverage except for a regular coffee. I arrived at the front of the line where the barista was ready to receive my order. I sheepishly asked if they had a regular coffee.

Recognizing that I was just a straightforward and simple coffee drinker, she gave me a smile and asked, "small or large?"

"Large," I responded.

She then proceeded to cock her head to the right and yell over her shoulder, "Large drip!" and then directed me to where I could wait for my beverage as she summoned the next customer. I waited patiently for a few minutes until my name was called.

"Large drip for Sean!"

I happily accepted my beverage from a partially shaved man wearing a black tee shirt with his hair tied back in a bun. I could never imagine pulling off that look in my relatively "strait laced" life. However, he matched the ambiance of the coffee shop. It was more than a place to just buy coffee. You could do that at any drive-thru chain. This was a place where your worries evaporated at the door and you could be transported to a warm and cozy world where everything was peaceful and carefree. That is, until you pay over five dollars for a cup of coffee. Then you quickly realize that the ambiance is not free!

I figured I would wait outside for a space to open up. While I was in the coffee shop, Monica had texted me that she was running about twenty minutes late. It was no worry for me. I felt like this discussion was the most important and nerve-racking thing that was happening in my life on that late Sunday morning. I did not mind the wait.

As I found a spot to lean against a tree and relax while I waited for Monica, my phone began to vibrate in my pocket. I checked it to see Christy's name on the call screen. I had been so preoccupied with my chili and coffee plan that I completely forgot that her flight would be landing in Florida around that time. I figured Christy would know something was up if I did not answer. I also realized I had about a fifteen-minute window now, but once Monica arrived, we would probably talk for an hour or so. Furthermore, I knew Christy had a busy afternoon and evening once she arrived at the Florida resort and conference center.

I did not want to decline this call and be a "bad husband." I did not want to give her any last-minute justification for her behavior.

I wanted her to do everything she was about to do with Matt knowing full well that she had a loyal, loving and good husband at home. I decided to answer and make her lie to me once again.

"Hey, did you make it?" I asked Christy as I answered her call.

"Oh yeah! It is beautiful and warm here. My flight landed a half hour early so I am already in the rental car. I should be getting to the resort in about twenty minutes!"

Her tone was full of anticipation and excitement, undoubtedly fueled by the warm breeze blowing through the palm trees which lined the street that led to Matt. My responses, in turn, were filled with a strained suppression of cracking and quivering.

"Is the team already there?" I asked.

"Yep, everyone is here! What are you up to today?" She inquired into my day.

I responded, "I think I am going to head to Rob's for that watch party for the game tonight. He is doing a chili cook-off, so I am making my green chili. Figured I would squeeze a run in while it's cooking."

I could hear the hum of the road against the tires through Christy's speaker phone as she replied, "Oh fun! Tell everybody I say hello and sorry I cannot make it. Have a great time babe! Okay, I have to go, I am about to exit the highway and need to figure out where I am going! But I hope you have a great time at the party. I will be really busy tonight setting up for the morning sessions so I probably will not get a chance to call tonight. I will talk to you tomorrow if that is okay?"

Her tone was so natural and so innocent. The depth of her deception did not seem to faze her. She knew she was lying to me. What she did not know was that I knew she was lying to me. She was too "busy" to call later. I guess it would be inconvenient to call your husband while your legs are wrapped around another man.

"It is amazing how you are able to juggle everything," was my attempt at blatant irony in response.

71

I continued, "Well, good luck with everything and I'll talk to you tomorrow."

I hung up right after that. It is amazing how the conversation was so normal, but the context had changed so much. I thought back to a line in the text message that Matt had sent Christy the day before. The one where he said, "I get to let all those feelings out with you (don't worry, I'll wait until after the SB for some of them)."

What a crass prick. But now I could not get the thought out of my head that while everyone watched the big game that night in anticipation and excitement, I would be counting down the minutes until the game ended, imagining Matt and Christy sneaking to one of their rooms after the game so Matt could "let his feelings" out with her.

-11-

Now Someone Else Knows

After hanging up the phone with Christy, my mind was racing with images of her and Matt. In about twenty minutes she would arrive at the resort and conference center. I imagined her walking in and catching a glimpse of him and the rest of the team. I imagined them sneaking rye smiles at each other while they longingly anticipated the moment they could finally be all alone.

Was it the thrill of sneaking around? Was she doing it to feel valued by a superior? Did she care that Matt is almost twenty years older than her with a wife of over fifteen years along with three great kids between the ages of seven and thirteen? How were they so reckless?

Matt is the Director of Human Resources and Christy was a Specialist in one of the departments he oversees. Christy's sense of self identity had been almost exclusively tied to her career in her adult life to this point. If their relationship were uncovered, it would surely have catastrophic consequences for both of them. How was she so comfortable living on a knife's edge while carrying on her foolish affair?

It was hard not to imagine them finally getting into a private room together. The images of them falling into bed as he kissed her and peeled her clothes off started playing like a bad movie in my mind. It was the type of consumption of thought where your eyes are open, but you do not actually see the world around you. All you see is the nightmare playing in your mind as your waking eyes strain to bring you back to the reality of your physical environment. I was internally pleading for something to snap me out of this trance.

Do you ever have that sixth sense that someone is watching you? That unexplainable impulse to quickly turn your head to confirm whether you have caught someone's gaze. Usually, this feeling is accompanied with a startled or shocked reaction. However, in this case, it provided a reflex that allowed me to escape the mental rabbit hole in which I had descended. Mercifully, the horrid image of Christy's ecstasy while she lost herself with Matt in his hotel room ended abruptly as I turned around just as Monica exclaimed, "Hey Sean!"

She was still a half a block away, but she had such a big smile and happy demeanor about her that I could not help but return a genuine wave and smile. Monica is one of those people who just has a cheerful way about her that is infectious and contagious. Sure, I was nervous and conflicted about telling her and the potential "can of worms" I was about to open, but it was honestly just nice to see a friend. It was nice to genuinely smile for a split second.

"Hey Monica!" My greeting was cheerful.

I continued, "The line is pretty long inside, I will see if a spot opens up out here while you order."

Monica acknowledged and walked inside the cafe to grab a hot tea. After a few minutes, some Adirondack chairs in direct sunlight opened up. I had been eyeing them for a while as the couple who had occupied them seemed to be wrapping up their visit. As soon as they started getting up, I was on my approach, ready to swoop in as the opportunity allowed.

With the optimal outdoor seating secured, I waited patiently as Monica ordered her tea inside. How would I start the conversation? Should I just get right to the point or should I suffer through the customary small talk pleasantries? Since Monica had just run a 5K in the park on that beautiful Sunday morning, I figured it would at least be polite to start the conversation with a discussion of the race.

With her tea in hand, Monica took a seat in the chair I had secured for her. Our chairs were situated at about a forty-five-degree angle with a little bistro-style, circular table between them. In keeping with the cafe's cozy theme, the outdoor furniture was an eclectic mix of patio furniture you would expect to see if you raided the garages of all your friends' grandparents. I was sitting in a plastic red Adirondack chair, while Monica was in a slightly smaller style made of wicker. The bistro table was awkward in that it was just a little too short for the chairs with which it had been paired. It also had a fascinating patchwork of weathered and chipped white paint that randomly unveiled the once concealed cast iron underneath.

I decided to immediately start the conversation before Monica had a chance to inquire as to why I needed to talk.

"How was the 5K? A lot of people?"

I went with the strategy to skip small talk and lead with the topic that was immediately relevant to her. It was also something I was genuinely interested in as an avid runner. I cannot deny that my mind was already thinking about all the random activities and races that may fill my time if Christy and I were to split because of the affair. I might as well get some feedback on this 5K, right?

Monica took the next few minutes to describe the event. It was more of a social gathering than a race. About a thousand people, all dressed up in their favorite professional football team's gear. There was music, beer, and pick up flag football games galore. It actually sounded like a lot of fun. It gave me a little glimmer of hope for exciting possible events that might be part of my rebuilding phase after the dust settled.

However, my transformation to another time and emotion was short lived. I was in the throes of survival and nowhere near any semblance of a recovery phase. I listened politely as Monica finished describing her experience.

"Yeah it was a lot of fun! You and Christy should do it next year! Anyway, what's going on with you?"

The moment had arrived. There was no way I could sidestep it and say something trivial like "not much." Monica knew there was something major we had to talk about. Why else would I have reached out and sent a message that I needed to talk before nine in the morning on a Sunday? My throat clenched up and I felt my body starting to shake as I choked out what I had met her to say.

"Well, I found some messages on Christy's phone. I don't know for sure, but I am fairly certain that she is having an affair."

My voice cracked and I felt my diaphragm convulse as my eyes welled up with tears while the words came out of my mouth. I felt so embarrassed. I mean, I was in public. I tried to keep my composure as best as I could. Monica certainly did not deserve to sit next to such an outlandish public display of emotion. I owed her that and so much more for meeting up with me to hear what I had to say.

I paused and gathered my emotions, as well as control of my breathing.

"Deep breath in. Slow breath out," my mind seemed to tell my body at a three second cadence.

I continued calmly and proceeded to explain the content of the text messages I had found. For additional context, I explained that Christy used to report directly to Matt and that he had been promoted in the last year to be Director of Human Resources. A description of her business trip to Florida and the nature of her request to extend the trip a few days for some personal time followed.

Monica listened patiently and intently as I described the timeline of the previous day's events. Monica had just seen Christy and me for the brewery and ice-skating adventure the day before. I explained that I had this knowledge in my head the whole day. I apologized for being disingenuous if it seemed like I was absent, or if my mind was elsewhere during that time. I talked about taking Christy to the airport that morning and the narrow escape of a devastating car accident. I told her all of this as a lead up to my ultimate request of the conversation.

I pulled out my phone and scrolled to the photo I took of the messages from Matt on Christy's phone. I asked her if I was misreading the text messages I had discovered. Then I handed the phone to Monica. She took her time to read the content a few times.

Then with a sigh, she looked me straight in the eye and said, "Sean, I am so sorry."

I could see it on her face and hear it in her voice. The messages were black and white with no interpretation needed. Christy was having an affair. It took the confirmation of a neutral party like Monica to actually make that reality sink in. I had been wavering for the last twenty-four hours about the level of deception Christy had been engaged in. I had given her the benefit of the doubt in some moments and severe damnation in others. I knew for sure that Christy and Matt were acting egregiously and inappropriately, but it was Monica's very somber and quick reaction that sealed it. There was no second guessing. There was no further analysis needed. Christy was having an affair with Matt.

The full nature of the affair was still in question for me though. Was it just an emotional affair? Maybe they had fooled around but had not had sex yet? Maybe their plan was to have sex that night to finally take their relationship and affair to that level?

I posed these questions to Monica.

She responded with a question of her own. "Sean, do you think he would have texted the things he did or expressed the way he loved her if they had not already been sleeping together?"

It is always amazing how a little outside perspective can provide such clarity to an internal debate that is raging inside of your mind. Monica's simple inquiry put to rest a question I had been wrestling with ever since I saw Christy's phone the previous morning.

We continued to talk for a bit. We actually managed to change the topic for a few brief moments. It was kind of nice to get the information off my chest and then just talk to my friend about something else. About an hour passed by and we decided to part ways for the time being. Monica would be at Rob's house that night for the party as well. As we rose from our chairs, she leaned in and gave me a warm hug. Then with a concerned voice, she looked me in the eye and asked in a very commanding voice, "So, I'll see you at Rob's later. Right?"

"I'll see you there." I then turned and started to walk back home.

-12-

The Big Game

I will be honest. It felt good to tell Monica what I had discovered. It felt good to get support and confirmation that what Christy had done was wrong and it was okay for me to feel devastated. It also felt good to have someone express understanding about my need to process first before impulsively acting. We are so accustomed to seeing tabloid headlines and trashy television shows about catching cheaters in the act, that it has shaped us as a society to believe that the only appropriate response to the discovery of an affair is to immediately confront the offender, tell them off and abruptly end the relationship. It is dramatic and it is entertaining.

However, it was not my reality. I will always be thankful to Monica for simply understanding and listening. She did not once try to tell me what to do or provide hypothetical advice under the heading of "Well, if it were me."

As I walked back to my condo from meeting Monica at the cafe, my mind went back to the image of the scene that was likely playing out in Florida between Christy and Matt. Monica's confirmation and support, while validating and encouraging, also brought the brutal reality of their affair into sharp focus. All the sudden, the timeline of Christy's day was very straightforward. I began to process how the events of her day would coincide with my own.

Christy had arrived at the resort to see her entire team who had just traveled together from New Jersey. Matt must have flown down with the rest of the team as well. I am sure they were all excited to see Christy when she walked into the resort lobby. They likely greeted her with smiles and hugs. Christy and Matt probably exchanged a romantic glance but had to keep up appearances of professionalism in front of their colleagues in order to conceal their affair.

In the time while I was talking to Monica and subsequently walking home, she had probably gone through the check-in process at the hotel. After she dropped her bags in her room, I am sure she was hurrying back to the hotel lobby to meet up with the team for any pre-game activities. They probably would coordinate the meeting room setups and last-minute talking points in advance of the next day's meetings.

Later, I would meet up with some of my friends back at Rob's house for the party. At that time, I imagined Christy would rendezvous with all the company managers at the hotel bar and join in the festivities centered around watching the big game. Her company had asked all the managers and superintendents from around the country, who were mostly male, to attend a meeting that began on the Monday morning after professional football's biggest day of the year.

I can only imagine that traveling for work on Super Sunday was not the most popular business decision with this crew. There would likely be a raucous crowd of disgruntled meeting attendees gathered to take in the game at the hotel. Christy's role was to facilitate the meetings of this retreat alongside Matt and the rest of the team, so I am sure they would be working the room as diligently as politicians looking for support.

Then the game would start. I would be mingling with friends at Rob's house, trying to keep my mind occupied and to be present. Christy and Matt would likely find times to touch base during the game. They would probably coordinate their plans to retire for the evening from the watch party. I was sure they would state their intentions under the guise of preparation for the next day. I just wondered how long they would hold out during the game. If it were a blowout, would they simply excuse themselves right after halftime? What if it was an instant classic? Would they have to endure sitting through the whole game until almost 10:30 PM Eastern time?

After the game, I would return to my condo. It would be dark and empty. I would crawl into bed alone. Meanwhile, Christy and Matt would be in the midst of their passionate reunion. How would they work the logistics? Would they use his room? Her room? Would they spend the night together, or would one of them leave in the middle of the night, making sure that no one saw that they had been in a room together?

This mental itinerary of the day became all consuming. It was like waiting for any big event. You know that the anticipated moment will come as sure as the sun rises and falls each day. At T-minus zero, the rocket will launch. There is nothing you can do, but just wait in anticipation as the time slowly ticks away. Monica had provided confirmation that Christy and Matt were having an affair. However, it seemed very symbolic to me that this was the first time that I knew about how the two of them would carry it out. I knew what they were doing and all I could do was wait. I did not even think confronting her would change anything at this point. It probably would just reinforce her desire to make the most of the night with Matt. Our marriage and relationship, as we knew it, had passed the point of no return.

Once again, I had allowed my mind to drift into the space of all-consuming thought of Matt and Christy's affair. At this point in my story, I had not even processed what to do about it yet. This mental boomerang was not going to end any time soon either. It was like being caught in a series of large waves out in the ocean. First a wave of emotion lifts you up and you can see the shoreline. You can see your escape. The wave is gentle at this point. It slowly lifts you up as you begin to formulate a plan for how you will make it to safety.

But then the wave begins to crest. You try to fight it, but the harder you fight the more energy you expend. Then the shoreline rapidly disappears as the wave grabs you and plunges you down to the depths. All the energy you burned trying to fight the wave leaves you breathless and panicked. As you tumble under the water, it is a struggle to regain your bearings. It is a struggle to determine which way will lead to the surface.

Finally, you see sunlight above you. You swim towards it with every bit of energy you have. As soon as you breach the water's surface, your body gasps for air. The air burns as it fills your lungs, but you are ecstatic because you made it to the surface. Thoughts of normalized breathing and the shoreline fill your head, if but for a brief moment. Then you look back.

"Oh shit!" you think. Another wave is bearing down on you. Having not even regained control of your breathing from the previous wave, you gasp deeply and prepare for the plunge.

This was my experience in surviving the immediate fallout of discovering what Christy had done. Unfortunately, it would be a theme for a long time to come. If I am being honest, it is one that I am still dealing with over a year later, only to a lesser magnitude. The harder I fought, the more difficult it was to recover. This was a hard lesson I had yet to learn.

I arrived home about forty-five minutes after departing the cafe. It took me a little longer than expected to walk home, so I was a bit short on time. This was probably a good thing. I did not have a lot of time to linger at my condo. Being in the Mountain Time Zone, the game started a little after four in the afternoon. But everyone would be gathering at least an hour or so in advance to start breaking the ice of awkward greetings that mark the beginning of a party involving professional adults. After a beer or two everyone would loosen up, the jokes and conversation would become ever so slightly less politically correct and the cheers would follow as the game commenced.

By this timeline, I only had about twenty minutes to get my act together when I got home. I quickly popped the lid off my chili and set the sauté setting to its highest temperature. I stood there and stirred vigorously as the stew bubbles let out an aromatic steam. After a few minutes, the concoction had reached a point of increased viscosity in which it slowly slipped off the spoon. I gave it a taste.

Yes! It was perfect. The flavor was bold, and the meat was tender. I grabbed a quick shower and ordered an Uber to take me over to Rob's house.

The Uber driver was a sweet woman, probably in her fifties or sixties. I was toting a large Instant Pot full of chili. I wonder what she thought as I walked towards the car with the slow cooker in hand. It suddenly hit me that someone may not love the idea of having a full pot of chili sloshing around in the back of their car.

I checked the license plate and we traded the customary rideshare name confirmation before I opened the door. I then noted that I was heading to a party for the game and the pot was full of chili. I noted that the lid was sealed, and I would keep it on the floor between my feet. I said all of this with a smile and fully anticipated that she may cancel the ride as it would be too risky to allow me to bring such an item along.

To my delight, she gave me a big smile and said that it was completely fine. She joked that she had driven many customers that day heading to parties with various food items and she was just taking stock of whose looked the best so she would know where to go for dinner after she was done driving!

After that initial exchange, it was a pleasant ride. The driver was a retired teacher. We engaged in superficial small talk on the way to the party. Weather and the current ski season were the topics that dominated the conversation all the way to Rob's house.

After ten minutes in the car, we arrived, and I thanked the driver again for her understanding in allowing me to bring the chili along.

As I stood outside of Rob's house, I could already hear the rhythmic hum of partygoers inside. Walking in the front door, there must have been twenty-five to thirty people already there.

"Hey Sean!" Multiple voices shouted. One of those voices was Monica. She was talking with several other members of the brewery running group. Rob greeted me and let me know where I could put my chili and my coat. There were several people who I had not met before. Many were personal friends and relatives of Rob.

As I walked into the kitchen to grab a beer from the cooler, it was akin to the receiving line at the end of a wedding. I met each person, one-by-one, as I walked through the kitchen. With each encounter, I tried to come up with a unique, ten-second, interesting anecdote.

By the third person, I had resolved to a simple, "Hey, I'm Sean. How's it going?"

After picking out an ice-cold beer from the fully stocked cooler, I retreated to the main living room with the television and the majority of the people I had known for longer than five minutes. The pregame commentary provided a muted soundtrack to the different conversations which filled the house. The place had an expanding energy as more and more people arrived. That energy then concentrated in the main living room as random party goers turned the surround system volume higher and higher as the chyron at the bottom of the screen noted something about the impending game that piqued their interest.

By the time Gladys Knight belted out the National Anthem, the room was packed with almost sixty people. The room fell silent as her voice filled the room.

"O'er the Land of the Free and the Home of the Brave!"

The room erupted with excitement and patriotism with those closing stanzas of our Nation's Anthem. My facial and body expression responded to the energy in the room, but my mind was on Christy. Matt had said that he could not wait for the game to be over to let his feelings out with her. The big game was about to start which meant in just a few short hours; Matt was going to be taking my wife to bed.

For football fans who remember the game in 2019, it was a bit of a defensive battle. In layman's terms, it was boring. The game featured the newly relocated Los Angeles Rams versus Tom Brady's New England Patriots. It was billed as the showdown of two high-powered offenses with wild predictions of record-breaking touchdown totals and points. However, let's just say the multi-million-dollar, cleverly crafted commercials provided most of the first half entertainment.

For me, the game clock provided a countdown to my biggest fear. By the time Adam Levine, of the band Maroon 5, was ripping his shirt off in the middle of the halftime concert performance, I had just two, fifteen minute quarters left until a man nearly twenty years older than me would sneak away and have sex with Christy.

The depth of despair I was feeling as I sat quietly on the corner of the couch came from so many places. For starters, I was emotionally devastated. The blind trust I had given as a husband to his wife was being blatantly violated without any regard.

I was also struggling on an elemental and instinctual level. I am a physically attractive, smart and emotionally intelligent man in my early thirties. The fact that Christy would rather be with an older man, with total disregard for his responsibility to his family, was like a sucker punch to the groin.

As the game resumed after the halftime break concluded, I felt my phone vibrate. Then it vibrated again a few more times. The source was text messages from Christy.

"Hey! Hope you're having fun at the party!"

"This game is super boring, but the halftime show was pretty cool."

"Good crowd here and everyone seems excited to be together for the meetings... YAY!"

"I think I am going to head to bed so I can get a bright and early start in the morning. Please do not worry about stepping out to say goodnight, I'll just talk to you tomorrow. Love you! Goodnight."

I felt my eyes cloud over. I sank deeper into the corner of the couch. I thought I had more time, but Christy was likely now leaving the hotel bar and heading to Matt's room, or maybe he was heading to her room. I guess it really did not matter. The specifics, which seemed so important to process earlier on, faded away as insignificant. The truth was that Matt and Christy were on their way to a night of passion together at a beachside resort in West Palm Beach, Florida while I sat on a couch at a friend's house in Denver.

Monica looked over to try and catch my attention. Without making a sound, she mouthed the words, "You okay?"

I shook my head no. Then I stared straight ahead. I watched the rest of the game. I smiled and responded when people talked to me. I drank a few more beers. I was pleasant enough to get through the rest of the evening. Eventually the final seconds ticked away in the fourth quarter. Patriots 13 - Rams 3. Tom Brady wins again.

I ordered an Uber from the app on my phone, collected my Instant Pot and thanked Rob for hosting the party. He did not say anything that night, but he has since told me that he could tell something was not right with me that day.

On my way out, I said goodbye to Monica and my friends. Tears filled my eyes shortly after I crossed the threshold onto the front porch. After an awkward minute or two standing alone on the sidewalk, my Uber pulled up. I was on my way home for the night.

-13-

Two Can Play This Game

It was nearly nine o'clock at night when I arrived back home after the party at Rob's house. Just fifteen minutes earlier, my surroundings included jovial people, postgame ticker tape on the television and upbeat music energizing the house. Now, back at my condo, my surroundings were dark, quiet and cold. I no longer had a crowd driven distraction to take my mind off Christy and Matt's current extra-curricular activities. My mind was fixated on images of the two of them together. The silence around me was deafening.

The next day I would have to go to work and figure out a way to focus. Maybe it would be helpful to go to my office and pour myself into work. I would be surrounded by coworkers and colleagues. Work would be able to provide another venue to escape my home and supply relief through distraction. I figured I would wake up early for a productive start first thing in the morning.

This was just another example of my avoidance strategy during these initial days after discovering the affair. I would identify a task, lose myself in anticipation of it, focus to the best of my ability once the task was at hand and then drown in the deferred emotion once the task had been completed. Then I would identify another task. This cyclical process had played itself out over and over since I saw Matt's messages on Christy's phone. Returning the phone to Christy's bedside table, the initial run, ice-skating, grocery shopping for chili ingredients, meeting Monica at the cafe, going to Rob's party, and now, work on Monday.

But there I found myself, alone in my condo. All around me were reminders of a life that was, while at the same time a life that is. I had entered a state of purgatory. I had no idea where life would take me from this point forward. But what I did know for sure was that the path forward was now drastically different than it had been just two days ago.

I was not quite tired yet, so I decided to crack another beer and watch some more of the post-game coverage. I kicked my feet up on the couch and tried to get lost in festivities being played out over a thousand miles away in Atlanta, Georgia. My gaze was on the screen and I tried so hard to focus on the specifics. As the Patriots collected their trophies and accolades, I tried to mentally break down the game and get lost in thought. I tried to force myself into mindless analysis of a game that literally had no direct impact on my life.

I tried, but it just was not working.

"Screw this!" I thought. "If she doesn't give a shit, then I don't give a shit."

I hopped up from the couch and decided that I was going out to a bar and my wedding ring would not be coming with me. It seemed like a reasonable and normal reaction.

"Two can play this game," I thought.

I had never taken a step outside of my marriage or ever truly contemplated it. Sure, there have been plenty of times where I have caught the eye of someone else throughout my adult, married life. I am a physically fit, reasonably attractive and steadily employed guy.

However, I had always been extremely quick to politely dismiss attention from anyone else but Christy. I would express a certain level of flattery, flash my wedding ring and strategically steer the interaction towards the topic of my marriage. As an example, if I was in a situation where an interested person had a recommendation for a new restaurant, I may have said something like, "You know what? That is a great suggestion. Maybe my wife and I will look into that!"

I was a loyal husband and generally would do my best to avoid situations in which temptation could creep in. I did not need the flattery. Being honest, I feel like I am a pretty confident guy. Not in the sense that I have an overt confidence, but more of the quiet kind. It is that quiet confidence that allowed me to be steadfast in my decisions. I made a commitment to Christy to be a loyal and trustworthy husband. I liked being a reliable husband and partner. I did not need validation from anyone outside of my marriage. The idea of even contemplating an extra-marital affair felt like an action so abhorrent and morally depraved. Not to mention, it felt like engaging in an affair would be more emotionally, mentally and physically exhausting than it would ever be appealing.

I also just never thought I could have an affair from the standpoint of my affinity for honesty and transparency. Anybody who knows me personally also knows that I have a terrible poker face. I like to be a genuine person. The idea of carrying on an affair would mean betraying Christy's trust. It would mean I would have to look her in the eye and lie right to her face. She would look at me as the person with whom she had planned all her life's hopes and dreams, while I would be looking at her as an "option." I do not know how anyone could live like that. Aside from not having a desire to cheat on my wife, the stress of living a double life seemed like it would have induced a crippling stress from which recovery seemed impossible. I could never do it and I never thought she would, or could, either. I guess I was wrong.

But now that I knew I was wrong to have thought Christy not capable of such a betrayal, I had a natural competitive instinct come over me. If Christy was capable of it and had no problem with having sex with Matt behind my back, why should I care about being a loyal husband to her anymore? It would seem I was totally justified in this way of thinking.

First off, she had committed this betrayal of our marriage, not me. She decided she was not satisfied with the life she had committed to and took selfish action to get more on the side, not me. She decided that her happiness resided in kindling a passionate love affair, but not with me.

Why should I give a shit about continuing as a faithful husband to an unfaithful wife? The moral hurdles seemed to get shorter and shorter as I leapt across them with each self-justification. I was going to go out. I was not going to seek to find someone with whom to "get back at Christy." However, I was not going to stop it if it happened. I was simply going out and putting myself out there. Tonight, I decided I was no longer married and did not have to answer to anyone. For all intents and purposes, I was just a single bachelor going out to a bar.

I was going out alone. Not only because the only person I had told so far was Monica and I did not want to tell anybody else yet. But also because I had never done this before. I had never gone out to a bar with the actual possibility of flirting with someone, hitting it off and picking her up. I had been with Christy since I was sixteen years old. This was all very new territory. I would probably be pretty bad at it and just wanted to be alone in the company of strangers.

Because I was alone, I figured I would need to find someplace that had some kind of event I could attend. After all, it was a Sunday night with most bars having just hosted events centered around the game. The crowds at those places were likely dying down and what would I do, go sit at the bar, order a drink and say, "Hey, I am here for the sweet post game analysis?"

I needed a better plan than just picking an ordinarily happening bar. I took out my phone and looked up establishments that had live events. Music, comedy, slam poetry, magic, whatever. It really did not matter. I just needed some sort of draw that would provide cover for why a guy in his thirties would go into a bar on a

Sunday night and sit down alone without looking as awkward as I felt.

Open Mic Comedy Night. Perfect!

I knew the bar where it was being hosted as well. I had been there several times as it was in my neighborhood. It had a really neat vibe about it as it was also attached to a coffee shop and bicycle repair shop. All three of the stores shared the building and its facilities, so there was a bond between them. They all played off the bicycle theme. You could meet up on a Saturday morning coffee before your ride, then afterwards, grab a beer with your fellow cyclists while the repair shop worked the kinks out of your derailleur and switched out your chain.

On this particular night, the Bicycle Beer Hall was hosting the Open Mic comedy event. This was a roaming event which seemed to pop up in various venues around the neighborhood. I had attended this event at other bars before. It was a familiar cast of characters. One comic provided a warmup act and then became the master of the ceremony, introducing each amateur comic with a quick hitting one liner to whip the crowd into a frenzy right before his three-minute set began.

The talent ranged from true novices testing out the comedic waters, all the way up to headliners on the local comedy circuit who were testing out new material. Talent was quickly recognized, and the crowd was a true equalizer. Your reputation meant nothing and did not earn you any points. The only thing that mattered was whether you brought the laughs for your three minutes on that particular night. That was it.

Sometimes a first timer would absolutely kill, while an experienced veteran just could not land a joke. No matter what though, the crowd ultimately showed each performer the same respect at the end of his set whether the material drew roaring laughter or awkward silence. Most people in the crowd would only ever observe the performances of others, as the sheer terror of facing a crowd like that would be too overwhelming. I shared in the sentiment of most people.

The crowd on that Sunday night was a little lighter than usual as I walked in. I guess it made sense as most of Denver was probably starting to preemptively regret the hangover that would hit them the next morning after the big game. But still, it was a nice sized crowd.

One thing I had noticed about these Open Mic comedy nights is that the artists seemed to know each other and had their own community. Most of the performers sat together in the back corner of the bar while others were up at the microphone. It was easy to pick them out of the crowd as their attire was usually one of two types.

Either they were dressed in jeans with a nondescript black tee shirt or a wild outfit which bordered on a character costume to add a visual element to their shtick.

The bar had about eight to ten high top tables which could accommodate two to four patrons each. Additionally, there were a handful of lower tables which could be used by up to six people who did not mind getting a little cozy with each other. The bar area had about a dozen stools and represented my seating goal. My gaze was fixated on the bar area as I walked in the door, there were two open individual stools. Both were flanked on each side by either couples or men. Maybe one of the couples would leave or the seating arrangements may change. Either way, I decided to take the stool farther into the bar area to become fully ingrained in the experience with plenty of barriers between me and a quick exit.

I found myself slightly disappointed that I was not immediately engrossed in a situation where I could exercise my newly found freedom from my suddenly, one sided marriage. This disappointment was probably due to the instinctual wave of competitiveness that seemed to be taking over. As I quietly asked the couple sitting next to my desired stool if anybody was sitting in the vacant seat next to them, I reminded myself that my intention was not to go out and look for something, but rather just be open to the possibility if it happened to present itself. I took my seat and scanned the list of beers neatly drawn on the blackboard menu. I wanted something on the lighter side. My alarm would be going off at six o'clock the next morning and I did not need to make that already unpleasant experience worse by drinking a whisky barrel aged, 12.9% imperial porter!

A 5% ABV Kolsch would do the trick. I settled in and listened intently to the musings of the actively performing comedian. My attention was broken only to accept my beer from the bartender while I whispered, "Thank you. I will keep the tab open."

The first comedian I saw was a heavier man with a full beard. In a traditional comedic style, he used self-deprecation as a form of irony for his set. His jokes mainly centered around his attempts to pick up women and the trouble he was having because the type of woman he was attracted to were, according to him, out of his league. With a little bit of shock value and crassness, he primarily focused on his assumed place on the attractiveness scale of 1 to 10 as compared to those he tried to win over.

Comedian after comedian came to the stage and tried to find the catalyst that would send the audience into a laughing fit. The crowd was mixed between those who were immensely engaged in the performance and those who were half listening while socializing with those around them. The former tended to congregate towards the front section near the performers while the latter hung towards the back area, out of respect for the artists. I found myself perfectly positioned in the middle. I was close enough that I could focus on the acts as a solo attendee or I could easily strike up a quiet conversation with someone nearby.

Right after I ordered a second beer, the couple sitting next to me paid their tab and left. I now had two prime seats to my right. I began to wonder who would take advantage of the open seats. The stage and microphone were near the entrance to the bar with most of the upfront seats already occupied, so I figured that anybody who would likely take the seats next to me would be new arrivals. I continued to focus on the current comedian's performance while also keeping an eye on the door.

Curiosity was filling my mind as the next person who entered the bar would likely be sitting next to me. I felt a nervous energy around the notion of potentially engaging with a complete stranger. I felt an even more nervous energy around the possibility that this stranger would be an attractive woman. This energy was certainly exciting, but more importantly it was incredibly distracting.

In all likelihood, Matt and Christy were in the midst of their passionate reunion behind closed doors at the resort in Florida at that very same moment. I could have either sat at home driving myself crazy with thoughts of what they were doing together, or I could go to a bar and pretend to be single for a few hours. Out of self-preservation, I chose the latter.

-14-

Or So I Thought

A few minutes went by and nobody new had arrived at the bar. It was probably getting too late for anyone to just be starting the night anyway. I was about halfway done with my second beer and decided I would go home after this one. It was probably for the best. However, just as the logistics of ending my evening came into focus, I felt a tap on my shoulder.

"Hi. Is anybody using these two seats?" The question came from an extremely attractive brunette woman wearing a pink top and jeans. Right behind her was her friend. She was also pretty, but my attention was focused on the woman who asked the question.

I acknowledged that the two seats were open and the two of them sat down next to me. I had noticed the woman in the pink top when I walked into the bar, but she and her friend were sitting at a table with two other men. At first glance, it seemed that they were all together on a double date, so I did not think much of it. As the two women settled in at the bar, their conversation centered on how weird their experience was with the two guys at their previous table. From the sound of it, they were sitting there first and then the two men invited themselves to sit down and proceeded to hit on them for the next forty-five minutes. When the women saw the couple leaving, they saw their chance to get away. Hence, they were now seated next to me.

Again, my intention was not to go looking for anything, but rather, simply experience an evening of what I suspected could be my new "normal." The two women were engrossed in their own conversation as they placed their beer orders with the bartender. I quietly sipped my drink and kept my focus on the emcee who was introducing the next stand-up comic. As the entertainer made his way from the back of the hall to the stage, I decided I would give this scenario a chance and ordered a third beer. I mean, why not?

The nervous excitement of a possible flirtatious encounter with the woman in the pink top seemed to fade over the next few minutes. I did not have much experience in this arena, but I was fairly sure that men are supposed to make the first move with a smooth opening line, usually in the form of an open-ended question to spark conversation.

However, I really did not have any intention of making a move. This was primarily because I thought it would be severely disingenuous to initiate with someone under the conditions of my current situation and secondly, because the sheer thought of starting a conversation with this beautiful stranger scared the shit out of me!

I resolved to mind my own business and take in the show as if it did not matter who was sitting next to me. The two women continued their conversation when there were breaks in between comedic acts and then their focus turned to the stage as the next performance fired up. During the actual performances they were respectful and kept any minor conversation to a soft whisper as to not impede the experience of anyone else. The two of them really seemed like they were just nice, polite people out enjoying a pleasant Sunday evening out on the town.

The woman in the pink top had a jacket draped over the back of her barstool. It seemed to be slipping off the chair ever so slightly, but it was not until she went to reach for something in her purse that the coat dislodged from the backrest peg nearest to me. In a reactionary way, she quickly put her purse aside to adjust her coat before it completely slid off the stool. As she made this adjustment, her leg swung around and brushed against mine.

"Oh! Sorry about that!" She quickly exclaimed, somewhat embarrassed.

"Please don't worry about it!" I responded.

We exchanged a smile as she fixed her coat and completed the task of procuring the lip balm from her purse. That was the extent of our exchange as we both regrouped and went back to watching the performance.

The emcee returned to the stage and announced that there was only one performance left.

"We are almost done up here for the night, but make sure you stick around and take care of our amazing bartender, Jill, after the show!"

It was a nice nod to the great service Jill had been providing all night. She was constantly leaning across the bar, straining to decipher orders which were being whispered to her over the hum of the crowd and the comedians' amplifier. She was working the bar by herself and no one in a crowd of nearly fifty people seemed to have to wait for a drink longer than a few seconds all night. In acknowledgement of this, the entire crowd, including the women next to me at the bar, turned towards Jill and gave her a round of applause.

After clapping, I put one hand on my beer and turned back towards the stage. To my surprise, I felt a hand on my shoulder as I turned.

"Hi! Do you know if they have this show here often?" The woman in the pink top asked me as the crowd settled back in.

I immediately felt my stomach knot up and my heart rose in my throat. I know it sounds ridiculous, but I had not had a conversation with an attractive woman from the position of being a single man since Christy and I had broken up for a year in college.

"I think the show rotates a bit around a couple of different bars in the neighborhood. This is the first time I have seen it here though." I responded to her inquiry.

She responded with excitement, "Well this is so much fun! My friend and I came out tonight just planning to have a quiet drink or two and stumbled upon this show. I definitely would go see this again!"

She continued, "I only moved to Denver a few months ago so I am excited to explore all the city has to offer."

Right after she made this statement, she immediately fell silent as the final act took the stage. It was like when the waiter comes to your table to refill the water at a restaurant. You could literally be in the middle of discussing a cure for cancer, yet everyone at the table feels compelled to cease speaking until all the water glasses are refilled. We shifted our focus back to the stage to enjoy the final performance of the evening.

As the performance ended, I decided to lean back into the conversation.

"So, you just moved to Denver? Where are you from originally?"

In recent years, Denver had become a city in which many people were moving to from different parts of the country. It had become quite commonplace when meeting someone new to ask her where she was from originally. Seemingly nine times out of ten, the person you were talking to had moved to Colorado from out of state.

"Wisconsin, right outside of Madison." She answered.

She then continued, "I'm absolutely loving it here! I was expecting the winter to be brutally cold, but this is nothing compared to Wisconsin. I cannot believe I was able to wear a tee shirt outside yesterday. In February!"

Many young adults in that current transplant wave seemed to hail from the upper Midwestern United States. It was also a quite common theme for Colorado transplants, particularly those who took up residence in the metro area of Denver, to be pleasantly surprised by the temperate conditions and ample sunshine during the winter.

Then she fully turned to me and stuck out her hand.

"I'm Amanda." she proclaimed as I reached out and shook her hand.

"Nice to meet you," I replied. "My name is Sean."

She then introduced me to her friend who had been sitting next to her at the bar.

"This is my friend Rebecca, she recently moved here as well from Texas."

Rebecca and I quickly exchanged greetings then she quickly turned back to a conversation she was involved in with another patron.

Amanda and I went on to chat at length about our motivations to move to Colorado. We chatted about our shared affinity for physical fitness, breweries, hiking, adventuring in the mountains and skiing. She was very beautiful and in incredibly good shape. She did not specifically mention it but as our conversation evolved, I was able to decipher that she was likely in her late twenties. She mentioned that she moved back home after college and started her career as a nurse at a hospital right outside of Madison. After about five years she decided to try something different, so she picked up and moved to Colorado.

She inquired about my motivations to move to Colorado and a little about my story. I proceeded to strategically omit certain details of my story by using the word "I" in place of "we" while I gave a little bit of my background.

I told her how "I" moved to Denver about three years earlier from New Jersey. I mentioned that "I" worked for an engineering firm in town and really loved how you could jump in your car from the downtown area and be lost in the Rocky Mountain wilderness in less than an hour. I mentioned that "I" initially moved to an apartment in the Ballpark District of the city but moved to the Capitol Hill neighborhood within a year of living in Denver. I talked about my love of the neighborhood that was a perfect mix of tree lined streets, residences, retail, restaurants and bars. It was also only about a fifteen-minute walk from the heart of downtown.

Amanda carried the conversation forward by explaining that she moved to one of the neighborhoods around Cap Hill somewhat sight unseen.

"I just decided to take a risk and go for it! I love my neighborhood though. I totally know what you mean with the amazing access to the downtown area while still feeling like a small-town neighborhood."

She described her somewhat free-spirited decision with an ear to ear smile. Her energy and jovial demeanor were infectious. Carrying on this conversation with Amanda transported my mind so far from the torturous thoughts of the activities that Christy and Matt were likely engaged in at that same moment in time. For that brief instance, I was present and in the moment. Amanda was engaged in a conversation with me and I was equally engaged in a conversation with her. The smiles, laughs and attraction seemed to be mutual and genuine. I felt free, if only for a moment.

We continued our conversation for another few minutes as we finished our drinks. Amanda then asked me what my plans were for the evening and if I would be interested in grabbing one more drink, perhaps at a different bar. This request, while extremely flattering and empowering, sent a gut punch of reality into my stomach and a wave of entrenched guilt consumed me.

I responded to Amanda, "I actually need to get home and get ready for my day tomorrow. I am actually married and just came out to have a drink or two and watch the show."

Amanda acknowledged and actually apologized to me for not realizing that I was married.

"Oh, no I am sorry. I should have mentioned that earlier." I assured her and continued as I paid my bill.

As I finished paying my bar tab, I continued, "I am so glad to hear you are enjoying your time here in Denver. I really enjoyed talking with you and definitely check out some of those places I mentioned. It was great to meet you!"

With that, I stood up and headed for the door, alone. As I quickly walked down the street back to my condo, my heart was racing so fast and beating so hard that I was convinced it might break through my chest. The lump in my throat was pronounced and my mouth was bone dry. My body started shaking. My hands started sweating. I felt that what I had done, simply having a conversation with another woman under the pretext that I was "single," was so beneath the promise I had made to Christy in marriage. My guilt was overwhelming. I really thought two could play this game, or so I thought.

I became perplexed. How could she cheat on me to an extent that was so complete, both emotionally and physically, while keeping a calmness about her as to conceal it from me? Yet, I could not even talk to another woman outside of our marriage without a physical manifestation of my guilt.

I walked into the dark and lonely condo. I contemplated how Christy could possibly do this to me. It seemed as if it would have been impossible for me to do the same to her. This thought consumed me. I thought to myself that there had to be something I missed. Something I just did not see or maybe did not want to see.

-15-

There Must Have Been Something I Missed

There was no way I could sleep on that Sunday night. It was nearing eleven o'clock and adrenaline was rushing through my veins. My flirtatious encounter with Amanda had sent my mind spinning. I just did not have it in me to go behind Christy's back, even though to the outside world it would have been completely justified and almost expected. But for me, it would have been a violation of her trust. I still cannot believe that is the way I thought about what ultimately amounted to a simple conversation with a woman at a bar. Even with the knowledge that Christy and Matt were likely in bed together at that very moment, I could not bring my own internal compass to grips with contemplating "cheating" on Christy, who was clearly in the midst of cheating on me with Matt.

Had I engaged in a continued conversation and possibly spent the night with Amanda, would that have even been considered "cheating" given the circumstance? Sure, if I did not level with Amanda about my situation and engaged in anything more under the context that I was a free and completely available man, I would have felt like a complete dirt bag, and deservedly so. But what if things had gone further with Amanda after I explained the situation? What if she had felt sorry for me and we continued our night together under the context of a mutual understanding of the situation, even if it was only for one night? Would that have been "cheating?"

In retrospect, I am glad that I had the sense to walk out of the bar and go home alone. But the experience certainly had me questioning previously held strong convictions of what is "right" versus what is "wrong." I felt like I was quasi-married. Did I have to live by my vows anymore? If Christy did not have to, then why should I?

I also was shocked at how I physically reacted to the thought that I was not being faithful to my marriage. Notice that I did not question whether I needed to be faithful to Christy, but rather faithful to the promises I had made, even if she was not faithful to the promises that she made. When I even contemplated enjoying the company and companionship of another woman, my body reacted to the feeling of wrongdoing and shame by shaking, sweating and other physical manifestations of stress. How in the world did Christy manage to avoid the overwhelming guilt, which had to be orders of magnitude more than what I had felt?

No one can be that good at hiding what they have done. No one can be that good at living a double life. As I paced around the condo, I looked at various items in our bedroom and closet. Christy's nightstand, her dresser, her stack of magazines, her bathroom drawers and her storage bins. I had never gone through her things in our marriage, but I quickly became consumed with the thought that her backstabbing deception had to have been right under my nose the entire time. There is no way she was that good at hiding. There must have been something that I missed and proceeded to ransack all her household possessions.

I started with her bedside table. I poured out the contents onto the carpeted floor. It was filled with a myriad of random items. Old receipts and airline boarding passes. There were candy wrappers from apparent late-night snacks. There were topical lotions, papers, pens and many other miscellaneous items. I went through them all.

In the dresser there was a stack of old Christmas Cards. Some of them looked familiar as they had been hung on the refrigerator in years past. There were several copies of the card that we had sent out several years prior. "Merry Christmas" with a picture of our dog sitting nicely on some fresh snow-covered grass looking directly into the camera. I remembered taking that picture, or rather the dozens of blurry outtake photos of the dog either not looking at the camera or facing away. I even remember the out of focus close-ups when she decided to abruptly lick my face and phone while I attempted to get one good photo!

I flipped through the stack of Christmas cards and found a few that I had not seen before. Many of them were cards given to Christy by various co-workers in her Human Resources department. Under a different scenario I would have thought of this collection of cards as nothing more than filing away some nice mementos of close colleagues. However, as I flipped through the stack, I just knew that there had to be one from Matt. Well I was wrong.

There was not just one, but three Christmas cards from three subsequent years, 2014, 2015 and 2016. There was not one from 2017 or 2018, which I thought was odd, given that it was currently February 2019 as I was rummaging through her bedside table, but at the time I did not think anything of those omissions.

The three cards from Matt prominently featured Matt's wife and three kids. Each card had a similar style. They were bi-fold cards, each with a large family photo on the front. On the back of the cards, there were individual pictures of each of Matt's children. Then on the inside front cover of each card was an annual family update noting Matt's accomplishments at work, his wife's projects around the household, notes from a family vacation and updates on the kids' school progress and sports. On the inside back covers was a simple holiday greeting accompanied by hand-written signatures from each member of the family.

It made me sick to see these cards. It made me sick to look at Matt's beaming smile as he embraced his family in the pictures. I could not stop thinking about his poor wife and those kids. How was I supposed to disclose what I knew? Christy and Matt had now put me in the position of not only dealing with my own emotional distress of their affair, but how my decisions and actions moving forward would have a direct impact on the future of Matt's family. Matt's wife is an adult and can handle this information in her own way. But the thought of those kids losing their father was more than I could bear. Matt and Christy were being selfish cowards. How dare they!

I flipped through the cards of Matt's family in chronological order, which had started with the 2014 Christmas card first. The 2015 card followed a similar format. I read every word and contemplated every picture. The sorrow for his family recycled in my mind all over again. Finally, I moved on to the 2016 card. I held the bifold closed as I looked at the family's cover picture. Then as I went to open the card, a piece of printer paper fell out. It had been folded in half with the blank side facing out, but I could tell there was typed print on the inside.

The paper contained a note of sorts. There were no formal names used, just "I" and "you" to denote the writer and the reader. It was about two-thirds of a page long. I could tell that it had significance right away. In reading it, I just assumed that it was a letter Christy must have written to Matt. The opening paragraph was a philosophical prose about the nature of being true to yourself and the happiness you derive from it. This was followed by a bit of text that was directed towards the reader.

I do not know how long this moment will last or if it is already gone. What I do know is that I will never regret it. I do not know what the future will hold for us or even if we will ever be together, but I am grateful that I experienced this time of pure happiness in my life.

The letter continued with a reference to a song that the writer claims to have always loved as one of her favorites. She uses the song to describe that the reader has always seen the writer for her authentic and true self. She then goes on to write a stanza from the song "Iris" by the Goo Goo Dolls.

And I don't want the world to see me. 'Cause I don't think that they'd understand. But when everything's meant to be broken, I just want you to know how I am.

Reading those words cut like a knife. The reference to the song "Iris" clearly had to have come from Christy. She loved the song and many of the other songs by the Goo Goo Dolls. I read those words and lyrics as some acknowledgement to Matt that there was a good chance they could not be together. However, Christy made it noticeably clear with her words and song reference that her time with Matt would be the pinnacle of love that she would feel in her life. According to Christy, Matt saw her in a way that she had never been seen before. He could see her true nature and that was something she had never felt before.

Here I was as Christy's husband, reading this letter to another man in which Christy confesses that the true authentic love in her life is not the man she married, but rather her boss' boss who was nearly twenty years her senior. The letter notes how well the reader (again, strong evidence that the reader was, in fact, Matt) listens and is compassionate. The reader knows how to say just the right thing, ask the perfect thought-provoking questions and listen with a superior emotional intelligence.

Again, Matt is the Director of Human Resources for their company and currently engaged in this fantasy laced affair behind his family's back as well. His entire professional career has been formed around the ability to practice active listening and right now his personal life was also clearly dominated by an infatuation with

Christy outside of his own marriage.

I will be the first to admit that I tend to avoid confrontation and am a bit of an analytical type. I tend to internalize problems and think about them to determine a solution that will both solve the underlying issue, as well as avoid making anybody feel badly or slighted. This may have come across to Christy in the past as being apathetic to what she was telling me.

However, what I would really be doing was thinking intensely about what she had said. This approach had created a tension in the preceding few years of our marriage. I am not perfect. I can easily admit that and had expressed to Christy on several occasions that I was trying to "get out of my head" and react to the conversation, even if I was not saying the exact right thing.

Well, Matt and Christy were both trained in the art of emotional intelligence and asking just the right question. Although Christy had only achieved a bachelor's degree in English, her career training seemed to have molded her into a second-rate psychologist of sorts. In her mind, she could detect strength and emotional intelligence in people. When the exercise of this perceived skill was accompanied by a man who knew how to ask the perfect open-ended and thought-provoking questions, apparently it was too strong of a force for her to resist. I was her husband because of relationship history and obligation. Apparently, Matt was her true emotional partner.

I placed the cards back in the drawer and continued rummaging through the pile of the drawer's contents. As I dug deeper, I saw a couple Moleskine notebooks. They appeared to be Christy's notebooks for work as they each contained her company's logo on the cover. When I flipped through them, I noticed that they were both completely filled with copious notes in Christy's handwriting. Each page contained a date in the upper right corner and based on these, it appeared the notebooks contained Christy's work notes ranging from the beginning of March 2018 through the week before Thanksgiving in November 2018.

The notes ranged from meeting notes to personal to-do lists. I had a feeling that these notebooks would provide a smoking gun regarding Christy and Matt's affair. Surely, in these notebooks, there would be some slip up where Christy must have written something about her relationship with Matt. Many of the notes seemed to be from her work trips to New Jersey when she went back to the company headquarter office.

She had typically traveled from Colorado to the New Jersey office for a few days at least once a month ever since we had moved to Colorado in 2016. Matt worked at the headquarter office. Each of these notebooks contained notes from occasions where she was in the same room with him, either in team meetings, or even one-on-one conversations. There had to be something in those notebooks.

Well, there was nothing. Not one small romantic or personal anecdote about Matt during their interactions. Not one mention of how he looked on a particular day or even a mention of a secret glance or smile. I even scoured the scratched-out notes to decipher the nullified text behind the random pattern of ink lines. Through all my scouring through her notebooks, it was all professional notes or innocuous personal musings. She was good. So far all I had were two text messages from Matt to her phone from Saturday morning. Sure, those messages provided evidence of her affair, but admittedly not much.

Before I put the notebooks back, along with the remaining contents of the drawer that I had dumped on the floor, I noticed a light purple booklet with a flowy, sketched outline of a woman's body. Below the sketch the title text read "Meditation Guide." I thought nothing of it. Christy had been meditating in the mornings before work. I thought it was because of work stress. I realized now that it was probably also due to the stress of living a double life, but it made sense. It must have been a small pamphlet on how to properly meditate and let her mind wander.

As I haphazardly returned all the items and closed the bedside table drawers, there were a few pens next to a couple of pill containers which appeared to be old prescriptions or aspirin. There did not seem to be anything out of the ordinary or suspicious about these final items I saw, so I moved to the closet. Then to her dresser. Then to her files. I was getting tired and really did not go through these locations and items with much depth. Mainly I just gave a cursory look without moving anything. There were a few suspicious items, but nothing conclusive. The only other item I found that night was a book in one of Christy's dresser drawers. It was titled "I Love You, But I'm Not In Love With You." As much as it hurt to see that book, it was not very surprising based on where we were. I did not have the patience or stamina to scour another couple hundred pages of writing, so I decided to move on.

At around one in the morning, I felt my eyes weighted with fatigue. With that, I suspended my search and went to bed. Over two hours of scouring the room with nothing to show for it. I set my alarm for six in the morning, less than five hours from the moment my head hit the pillow in my bed.

-16-

The Letter

Mercifully, I fell asleep rather quickly after laying down. I do not remember much after resting my head on the pillow. My fatigue had even prevented me from changing out of my jeans and settling in under the bed sheet and blanket. I had been running on such adrenaline from a whirlwind day that I think my body just needed to crash. It was like I was on a combination sugar, caffeine and drug induced high all day that culminated in a massive energy crash as I finished my first pass of Christy's belongings in the search for clues.

It was a deep sleep. One which was devoid of all cognition and awareness. The temporary mental reprieve was like a euphoria. My only sense of consciousness seemed to be reserved for the most basic functions which barely allowed me to be cognizant of how deeply I had drifted into my slumber. It was akin to a shot of morphine after an acute injury. When the pain you feel is overcome by the feeling of nothingness in its place, it seems like one of the closest things we can feel to Heaven on Earth.

In that euphoric state, my mind drifted into dreams. Those dreams must have wandered through story lines of fantasy and illogical thought at first. However, as in most dreams, our realities enter in to give the dream a sense of credibility in your mind. To bring the illogical thought into an uncomfortable purgatory in which reality and fantasy are interwoven such that you cannot decipher where one ends and the other begins. For me, the most prominent example of this reality-based dream state is a recurring dream I have tended to have throughout my adult life.

In the dream, I am back in high school. This is completely illogical because I am fully aware in my dream that I am a professional adult who successfully graduated high school, and subsequently, college. I can easily comprehend that it is a dream based on that premise alone.

However, as the dream progresses, I notice the details of my surroundings. The high school is my actual high school, with the setting replicated down to each exact sensory detail. The location of my locker, my classmates' faces, the layout of the building, the color of the carpet, and even the pitch of the bell signifying the start or end of class are all accurate in my memory of my experience.

I realize I am heading into a history class and there is one last exam before the end of the year. The location of the classroom is the same location as my real senior year history classroom. It is all the way at the end of the hall, last door on the left and just before the exit to a courtyard off the side of the building. The class is taught by my actual senior year history teacher. She gives me a confused look. It then hits me that I had not attended the class all year and I cannot graduate. The contextual reality, mixed with the fantasy induced stress, cause me to abruptly awake in a panic.

On this night though, it was not a failed high school class that haunted my dreams. It was Christy's relationship with Matt. My random dreams focused on a beach in Florida. From there, I could see a resort area with Spanish tile roofing and a white stucco exterior. It was set back from the beachside highway by a lush green and meticulously manicured lawn. As I walked toward the resort lobby, I heard a familiar voice, but the voice was not talking to me. Rather, the voice was accompanied with giggling and laughing. I turned around to see Christy in the arms of Matt as he embraced her and slowly kissed her neck. She must have noticed me, so she quickly shook Matt off her.

She looked me square in the eye and said, "Well now you know."

Then she and Matt walked off to get on the elevator to their room. In the dream, I was then teleported outside of their hotel room. I put my ear against the door only to hear them in passion and ecstasy. I felt myself hyperventilating and shaking as I began to open the door.

Almost immediately, I was awake again. I was lying in my bed back in Denver. Jeans still on and lying on top of the bed spread. My breathing was rapid. My heartbeat was racing, and I had a small tear dripping out the side of my left eye. I reached for my phone amongst the darkness of the room. Having secured it, I pressed the button on the side and the screen illuminated.

2:52 AM.

I slept for just a little under two hours. I tried to calm my mind, but it was of no use. Extreme fatigue may have won the previous battle against the persistent thoughts of Matt and Christy together after my search of Christy's possessions. However, those same thoughts had fought back to break into my dreams, overtake my subconscious reasoning and finally regain their place at the forefront of my conscious thinking upon awaking. I closed my eyes and tried to force myself to fall asleep. Twenty minutes passed and with each of them, adrenaline and stress increasingly replaced fatigue. By 3:15 AM, I was out of bed and completely awake.

With the prospects of getting anymore sleep completely obliterated and almost three hours until I was scheduled to wake up, I put on a pot of coffee. Sitting at the kitchen breakfast bar area during those early Monday morning hours, I started to contemplate how I would confront Christy about what I knew.

Her meetings were scheduled to be completed at the end of Wednesday. Then she would have her personal extension of the trip, which I had determined would likely be a romantic getaway with Matt. She was scheduled to leave Florida on Saturday morning and arrive back in Denver later in the afternoon that same day.

I contemplated just confronting Christy while she was in Florida. However, I did not really want to do it over the phone. I actually considered hopping a plane to Fort Lauderdale and showing up at the resort to surprise her in person and stop whatever she and Matt were doing. I went so far as to pull out my computer and start investigating plane tickets. It took a few minutes, but the reality of the logistics and cost of pulling off the trip, not to mention the shear manic nature of the thought of such a trip itself, veered me back to a sane line of thinking.

So, I decided I would wait until she arrived back in Denver. I would let her know that I would not be available to pick her up from the airport and she would have to take an Uber home. When she arrived home, I would not be there. Rather, I would make a hotel reservation to stay away from the condo for a few days.

What would be waiting for her at the condo would be a letter. A letter which would describe everything I found and everything I felt. It would detail my entire week of agony and turmoil while she basked in the Florida sun with her lover. I opened a word document on my computer and began at the beginning.

Christy,

I know.... I know... I KNOW! Betrayal, loneliness, extreme sadness, anger, regret, jealousy, nostalgia, fear, guilt, inadequacy, failure, sympathy, stupidity, disengagement, denial, and acceptance: these are just some of the words that describe what I have been going through over and over again since I found out. I have had physical manifestations of the unfathomable struggle of realizing that the person I love and trust more than anyone or anything, the person who promised that same love and trust to me, could possibly cause pain and betrayal worse than anything I have ever felt.

For a little while, I had noticed changes. It started with just a simple feeling of distance and lack of intimacy. I know this may sound ironic, because we have been struggling with regaining a passion and an intimacy back into our relationship. But this was different, I not only felt the distance, but also a sense of secrecy and avoidance. I mainly associated this with you being sick at the time. "Don't kiss me", "keep your distance", "I don't want to get you sick", these were justifiable in my mind and explained a deeper level of lack of physical and emotional intimacy, at least in a way that made sense to me in the moment. Then I noticed other things, mainly your attachment to your phone and an odd secrecy to your behavior around it. At first, I thought maybe it is just private discussions with your friend about her pregnancy and how she is feeling. Maybe she was entrusting you with some feelings or emotions she did not want shared. This seemed to make sense at first. But then it continued, I noticed that many times when we were in the car, an Uber, or just sitting on the couch, you would be typing away with the phone cupped in your hands so close to your face as to not allow anyone to see what your conversation was about and when I gave the faintest glance over, you would hide your phone. I noticed how you were spending much more time behind closed doors in our own home, mainly the bathroom. I attributed this to you not feeling well and tried to justify it away in my mind.

I could not take it anymore, I had to know. On Saturday morning, while you were sleeping in, I glanced at your phone. You had received a WhatsApp message overnight. A "heart" from Matt. My chest pounded and my breathing nearly stopped. For a split second, there was still a reasonable explanation in my head. You had shared a great idea for the Manager's meeting... you had shared that you had the pictures taken care of for your living room style program at the meeting... or any other number of logical and professional reasons. But then I noticed that the "preview" on your phone screen showed two messages were received. I scrolled to see the other message. What I saw caused one of the most devastating feeling I have ever felt...

"Soooooo close :D :D :D :D :D :D!!!!!! Only 1 more night to go!!! I'm out of my mind excited to see you!!! I keep thinking about being together and cannot contain myself anymore. You are the woman I want to take care of, touch, feel and be with and tomorrow I get to let all those feelings out with you (don't worry, I'll wait until after the SB for some of them ;)). I've missed you so much sweetheart!!! I love you Christy!!!! (6 winking kissy faces)"

I took a photo of the messages with my phone and collapsed onto the couch, hyperventilating and uncontrollably shaking. I was frozen. I knew I could not react in that moment because I was so far outside of my body. I walked back to the bedroom and placed the phone back on the table. I was shaking so bad that I dropped the phone on my first attempt to replace it.

I thought "OH SHIT!, don't wake up... I can't do this... please... I can't do this".

I placed the phone back and just stared for a few minutes. I stared at you, I stared at the phone and I stared into space. My mind was racing. My thoughts were incoherent and random, just filled with phrases from sheer disbelief to uncontrollable rage to crippling uncertainty.

"FUCK YOU!"

"HOW COULD YOU?"

"THIS ISN'T REAL!"

"MAYBE THIS IS SOME SORT OF TWISTED JOKE?"

"IT'S OVER."

"WHAT AM I GOING TO DO?"

In a ridiculous twist of fate, at that moment, my brother called. I was so shaky and out of my mind that I went to decline his call and instead accidentally answered. I could not even see straight and the room was spinning. Now stuck in a conversation where I had to fake everything was just fine, I stomached every urge I had to say, "I just found messages on Christy's phone, my wife is cheating on me." The agony got worse when he conferenced my mom in. All I could think about was this devastating revelation and how easy it would be in that moment to turn a peaceful Saturday into a horrible day. I had this overwhelming urge to broadcast what I knew to people I trusted, because the woman sleeping in the next room is no longer someone I trust.

I want you to know how horrible of a feeling that is. It is only out of respect for our relationship and my fidelity to you, to be true to you in good times and bad (words that ran through my head over and over and over), that I pretended to be fine, happy in fact and excited about our day of ice skating and friends. This was the first conversation in which I was now lying to everybody I loved.

At just after five in the morning, I closed my computer and took a break. My first work meeting of the day started at 7 AM and I had no idea how I was going to get myself into the correct headspace to get through that meeting, let alone an entire routine day of work and interaction with colleagues. I sat down on the couch with a fresh cup of coffee and turned on the morning news. In a fortuitous move, I decided to set an alarm for 5:50 AM. Just in case.

It seemed like my eyes were only closed for a split second when the alarm ring on my phone started blaring.

-17-

Back to the Grind

Monday morning was here. Over the course of the weekend I had maybe slept four hours total and now I needed to go into work and manage to be a functioning member of society. It was time for me to attempt to put aside my personal turmoil for the next ten hours. Somehow, I would have to find a way to manage to hit pause on my emotions and put in a solid day's work.

It was going to be a busy day. My first meeting of the day would be a weekly catch up with my manager, then I had about an hour after that meeting concluded before I had to give a presentation to a client across town. Between the travel between my office and the client's, along with presentation and follow up discussion, I would not be back at my office until nearly lunch time. In the afternoon, there were three separate project meetings I had to attend. Two of which I would be running. Amid all of that, I would have to find time to do "actual" work, document the discussion of each meeting and move forward or delegate any actionable items. It was going to be a busy day.

There is a certain cruelty to it, don't you think?

Christy had plenty of time to think about what she was doing. She had the benefit of gradually introducing the thought of having an affair with Matt into her life. She was able to weave that thought into her personal and professional actions at her own pace.

Me? I had less than forty-eight hours between discovering that my wife was having an affair and showing up for a 7 AM, Monday morning meeting which would kick off a rather busy workweek. It just did not seem fair. While my world stopped, everyone else's kept spinning. Now I had no choice but to clean myself up, fake a smile and catch up with the relentless march of time.

I arrived at the office around a quarter to seven to try and go through a bit of a normal routine before my meeting at seven. I dropped my bag in my office and immediately walked over to the kitchen. I must have been the first person to arrive on my floor as no one had yet made the coffee. Dark roast was my choice that morning and I brewed it extra strong. I was there first so I brewed the coffee I needed. It was the Monday morning after Super Sunday anyway, so I am sure everyone would probably appreciate a high-octane brew!

Back in my office, I waited as the coffee was brewing. I logged onto my computer and had a few minutes to spare. Luckily, I had been on top of my game with preparation of my presentation for our client across town later that day. I had actually finished the presentation and rehearsed it on the previous Friday. It turned out to be extremely fortuitous that I did not save this marketing presentation as one of those items that I would usually take care of on the weekend!

My mind was still burning with the idea of writing Christy a letter about my experience after discovering her affair. I was up to the part where I decided to go for a run and determine whether I would confront her that morning. Using my notebook, I jotted down some key reminder phrases like "Run around Wash," "Confront or not," and "One more day of normal."

There were about three minutes before the start of my weekly discussion with my manager. At about this same time, I figured the coffee would be about done brewing. I headed for the kitchen to pour a cup while I was on my way to my manager's office. To my surprise, my manager must have had the same thought. As I rounded the corner into the kitchen, she was standing there over the coffee pot.

"Hey Sean! How was your weekend?"

She asked the question in a way that was so energetic and full of excitement. It is a welcome, albeit abnormal, level of energy for an engineering consulting firm on a Monday morning. But whether she is feeling that energetic or not, the enthusiasm tends to be contagious and typically fosters smiles and lively conversations about weekend adventures before diving into business discussions.

With about as much energy as she asked her initial question, she subsequently continued before I could respond.

"We can probably just talk about it in my office rather than in the kitchen. Grab your coffee and I will see you in there!"

With that, she turned and walked out of the kitchen as I prepared my beverage. Dark Roast, half a container of single serve creamer and a pinch of sugar. With my coffee in hand, I was off to officially start my day.

I walked into my manager's office and took a seat at my typically location in a chair by the window. There is no agenda for this meeting as it is meant to be an open chat about what is going on in our work lives or personal lives. Although there is no standard format, our conversations generally tend to follow the same loose schedule.

We start off with about fifteen minutes of discussion about our personal lives. Then we will chat for about twenty minutes about a larger project that we both have been working on together. I will then proceed to go through the litany of projects that I am actively managing or working on separately, as well as talk about any upcoming marketing and business development opportunities. Finally, we will usually circle back on a continued discussion of our joint project if time permits.

As I entered her office, she asked the question again. "So, how was your weekend?"

I answered the way any twelve-year-old answers his mother when asked about his day at school. "It was good," I replied.

It was good! It quickly hit me that I had just answered an open-ended question with a closed response, which is just about the biggest gaffe you can make in a grown up, professional conversation with your boss.

I quickly followed up. "Yeah, the weather was absolutely beautiful. It felt great to get a run in on Saturday morning around the park and I had a great time with some friends to watch the game last night."

I strategically left out any mention of Christy or activities which had involved Christy.

"How was your weekend?" I quickly asked to stave off any follow up as my strategy was to attempt to get to the professional topics as soon as possible.

"It was great! My husband, son and I were able to take our mountain bikes out on Green Mountain! I honestly thought it would be too muddy and was nervous about beating up the trail, but it has been so dry lately that there was hardly any mud. We just relaxed at home for the rest of the weekend and just spent a quiet night in with the family to watch the game."

With her response, I tried to seize my opportunity to move the conversation towards our project. However, she cut me off and asked the follow up questions I had been dreading.

"How is Christy doing? She was supposed to travel this week to Florida for that big meeting, right? Did she make it in okay or have any trouble getting through the airport yesterday?"

I attempted to keep calm and maintain my composure.

"She is doing well. Yeah, her meeting with all the company managers is this week down in the West Palm area. She made it in yesterday and pretty much had to hit the ground running as soon as she arrived."

With that last statement about Christy's arrival in Florida, my voice started to subtly quiver and crack as I felt a tear start to well up in my right eye.

My manager pressed on. "Well that's good, were you both able to at least do something fun together on Saturday before she left?"

At this point my eyes must have started to get visibly bloodshot. My mind started scouring for the words to formulate a halfway decent response to her question. All I could think about were the text messages I had found on Christy's phone. I am usually particularly good at reserving myself to a well-crafted and filtered response. However, I blurted out exactly what I was thinking.

"I found out on Saturday morning that Christy is having an affair."

I was almost as shocked at saying those words as my manager was at hearing them. I immediately felt as if I wanted to suck the words right back into my mouth. I could not believe that I had just disclosed this level of personal information at my first meeting of the week in my workplace. To my boss, no less. My manager's face dropped. Her astonishment was painfully visible. Her exited tone immediately turned somber.

"My God. Sean, I am so sorry. Are you -? How did you -? Does she know that you know?" She did not have to finish each of the questions for me to know exactly what she was asking. She was genuinely inquiring about my well-being from a state of disbelief.

At this point, I had tears streaming down my face and shrunk into the chair. That morning I had worn my traditional well-fitting button-down shirt and tailored dress pants. Being a fairly fit individual, it is the type of outfit that tends to give me an extra boost of confidence. It is the type of look that helps me demonstrate that I am a bit of an authority figure within the company. That image evaporated in that chair in my manager's office. She closed the door and handed me a box of tissues.

I responded to her round of questions with the story of what I had found, my decision to not tell Christy yet and that she was only the second person that I had told. I disclosed that I had not even talked to any member of my family yet about it. All of her follow up questions started with a bit of a pause and a stammer. It was indicative of person who was struggling with an anticipated response before ever asking a question, similar to news reporters who are interviewing someone about a significant and raw story involving human tragedy.

She and I both knew that we were in a professional setting, but this information and ensuing discussion transcended typical professional filters. While not everyone has had infidelity happen to them, the suspected emotions around the thought of a spouse betraying their partner tends to strike a very visceral reaction in most people.

My manager then pivoted the conversation towards our company's commitment to me as a valued employee and what she could do to put me on a path for support. She encouraged me to talk to our Human Resources representative about support services that are included in our company's benefits. She also asked if I needed to take any time away from the office. To this I responded that I would consider it, but for right now I wanted to keep coming to the office to focus on work. My only other option would be to sit in the condo and stew in my own thoughts all day.

She then asked what my day looked like. I mentioned my client presentation across town. With a concerned look, she asked me if I could handle the presentation. To this, I replied that I could. It was a testament to her trust of my professionalism and ability to deliver that she allowed me to move forward with delivering the presentation under these conditions.

We had only used up about a half an hour of our meeting time, but the conversation came to a natural stopping point. I do not think either she or I had any desire to talk about actual project work. Without saying it, I think we both just had a mutual understanding that pivoting the conversation to project schedules, action items and logistics would be forced and inauthentic.

I asked her if we could table those topics for another time. I noted that I wanted to go run through my presentation one more time and start to investigate my benefits and resources before heading to the client meeting. She agreed and as I got up to leave the room, she made of point of reminding me that our company is like a family and that she would be there for me for whatever I needed.

After my meeting with my manager, time seemed to quickly pass by and before I knew it, I was sitting in my client's conference room with my presentation up on the screen. To everyone else in the room, it was just another Monday morning. For me, it was really time to put my personal dilemma aside and deliver a great presentation. Once again, it was time to perform. My character was the Sean that existing last Friday before the affair ever existed in my world. I stepped into my role and the presentation began.

From most accounts, it went well. I delivered the presentation as rehearsed and the follow up question and answer discussion was lively and thought provoking. For me, it was just thrilling to have it behind me. As my co-worker and I walked to the car to drive back to the office, he gave me a pat on the back and told me that he thought I had knocked it out of the park. The shot of confidence felt good. He had no idea how much energy it took for me to get through that meeting.

The rest of the day was fairly standard. I had many remaining internal meetings and random discussions around the office. It was a particularly busy day, so it kept my attention focused. I was appreciative of the busy nature of that day.

Around 4:30 in the afternoon, my last meeting ended. I had more work to do, but I was feeling very burnt out and the personal distractions were starting to take priority once again in my mind. I decided to call it a day and head home. My mission for the evening was simple. Run and write. Oh, and I should probably try to eat something and get some sleep as well.

-18-

There HAS to Be Something I Missed

After I left the office, I walked the eleven blocks back to my condo. Given that it was the beginning of February, the sun was low in the sky and I had less than an hour of daylight left. In stark contrast to my weekend runs during the middle of two abnormally warm days, this evening's run would be dark and cold. The temperature had already dropped below thirty degrees even with the remaining sunlight. Being that Denver is located in a high elevation dessert, the daily winter temperature tends to plummet as the sun begins to set.

Back at my condo, I changed into my running gear. Layering is the key for running in the cold, dry air of Colorado. First, I put on some running shorts and a technical tee shirt, over which I wore gray sweatpants and a green sweatshirt. Over the green sweatshirt was an old windbreaker from my first Boston Marathon. Finally, I doubled up with two pairs of socks under my blue running shoes, slipped on a pair of liners from some winter gloves, and pulled an old beanie over my head.

I was properly outfitted against the cold. But now it was time to equip myself with some illumination. The Boston Marathon windbreaker had some subtle reflective qualities, but it is in no way a safety grade reflective jacket. I supplemented with a headlamp over my beanie. The lamp shines a white light to illuminate the path in front of you, while a light on the back of your head flashes a deep red to alert drivers and other users of the streets and sidewalks of your presence.

With all my preparation against the elements complete, I walked to the door of my condo unit and grabbed the leash to take my dog out before my run.

As I looked back across the interior of my home from the entrance door, I pondered the silence and tranquility in my home. I was in such a rush to get back to the condo and quickly change for my run, that I hardly noticed the stillness in my home. Where Christy normally sat at the table during work hours was just a dark monitor with a few papers containing her handwritten notes. There were no dishes in the sink or murmurs from the television. Heck, when I had walked into the condo unit, I had to turn on the light because everything in the unit was beginning to be shrouded in darkness. My dog even seemed affected by the lack of activity, as my return to the condo was met with her stammering out of the bathroom from a long nap like a drunk.

I took my dog out for a quick walk around the block to relieve herself and then brought her back inside. This time, I decided not to linger for very long in my home. When I had noticed the stillness of my home before taking the dog out, it was more odd than depressing. However, it started to sink in while I was walking around the block that the stillness and quietness would be there when I returned. I would have to live in it with nothing but my thoughts if I did not come up with a distraction. There was a noticeable vacuum in my home. It seemed like the life that once inhabited it had died and all that was left was emptiness and the hum of the HVAC unit.

It was a cold, but such a beautiful run. Typically, this type of weather has me looking forward to completion of the run before I ever start. But given what I had to go back to, I savored the experience. For about forty-five minutes, it was nothing but my stride, my headphones and the sidewalk.

I took my typical weeknight route which loops around Denver's City Park. At the eastern end of the park, the route reaches its highest elevation. From there, just on the edge of the City Park Golf Course, you are treated to one of the most spectacular views of downtown Denver with the Rocky Mountains draped in the background.

It was an extra special treat that night as I had timed it perfectly to see the last hues of sunlight on the horizon silhouetting the majestic peaks. The skyscrapers in the foreground were filled with random office lights brilliantly beaming from their facades. There was still enough residual light on the eastern face of the mountains that you could still see the snowlines and striations on the massive rock formations. The sky framed the whole image with a soft fade from navy blue directly above me to a rose-colored gold just over the mountains. I stopped to take it in. It was pure beauty.

This spot marked the exact halfway point on my run. I just stood there staring off over the peaceful winter landscape. Up until this point in the run, I was running away from my condo and symbolically, my heartbreaking anxiety and loneliness. Every step I took away from that place gave me some sense of control over my situation. Each step gave me temporary relief and a renewed, yet faint, optimism that I would be all right. But as I have come to learn time and time again since that fateful Saturday morning, problems are not like fine wine. You cannot just run away and forget about them, hoping that they will get better. You must face them head on, digging and clawing your way to the painful root before you can begin to heal and move on.

There are countless self-help books and articles on facing your problems head on. I am sure almost everybody hears this advice at some point in their lives from a parent, sibling, spouse or a friend. For many people, I would venture to say that it is a mantra that they have heard repeatedly in their lives. I certainly have. My parents instilled a deep sense of personal responsibility in me. To do what you think is the right thing to do, even if it is the hard thing to do.

I had been very blessed that, up until this point in my life, I only ever really had to apply this advice to seemingly trivial problems. However, even in those applications where the short-term discomfort is extremely swift and fleeting, it can be extremely difficult to heed that advice. How in the world was I going to tackle this head on when I had never experienced anything even close to the level of difficulty in front of me?

Standing at the highest point of City Park, I was suspended at the tipping point of dealing with just one aspect head on. Should I keep running away or start on my return home? The journey back would lead me to a dark, cold shell of a life that was. All the pictures still hang on the walls. The furniture is in the same position. Our dog will greet me at the door as if everything is the same. That is because every "thing" in my life is the same at this point. The only change is that my life's purpose and meaning had been shattered.

However, the relentless truth of the matter was that no matter how far I ran, I would have to turn back. I took a photo of the beautiful mash up of landscape and cityscape before me and turned to continue down the sidewalk.

In the first half of my run, each stride brought increasing relief. As I ran home, the anxiety flooded in with each foot strike on the concrete. I could not run away from this. The only thing I could do was buckle up and try to hang on for dear life as my life was tossed around like dinghy in the middle of a hurricane.

Arriving back at the condo brought a notion that seemed to reinforce the fact that I could not escape this reality. Just like my current situation, the condo was exactly as I had left it before my run. I could have been gone for five minutes or five months, everything would have been exactly the same. I took off my outer layers that were still cold to the touch from the crisp winter air. Before I would sit down to continue writing my letter, I needed to take a shower to remove the chill from my bones.

The hot water initially stung my extremities as it cascaded over my body. It is an odd sensation. When your fingers and toes are so cold that hot water actually stings at first. It is like your body's way of creating a barrier to reinvigorate parts of your body that it seems like you have allowed to die due to the cold. However, as the stinging subsides, it is replaced by a soothing sensation as your extremities regulate themselves back to a state of normalcy.

As I stood there in the shower, I was trying hard to think about what I wanted to write in my letter to Christy that night. I wanted to determine how much I would write, what point in my narrative I would end for the evening, and to what level of detail would I go. I wanted to think about the writing process. It was mine and I could control it. However, these thoughts of my letter writing process kept getting hijacked by the notion that there was something in the house that I was missing. Something I would find that would both prove two things. First, that Christy was not as good as she thought she was about hiding her affair and second, that I should have never been so blind to what was right under my nose the whole time.

The thought was so consuming that I abandoned my intention of writing that evening. I convinced myself that I had plenty of time to write the letter before Christy arrived back home the following weekend. Instead, I was going through everything and I would not stop until I found something. I quickly ended my shower and changed into some fleece pajama pants and a tee shirt before I commenced my search.

I started with her closet again. I looked at every piece of clothing and checked the pockets of every single bag. For Christmas the past year, I had given her a new piece of luggage to make all her work travel easier. She was using that new bag on her current trip. The closet was like a graveyard of her outdated bags and luggage which had either exceeded their useful life or were replaced by a more useful carrier for her belongings.

I ripped into every pocket of her the last travel bag she used before switching over to the one I had purchased for her as a gift. It was a duffle with a bunch of random letters in random colorful patterns on its surface. In this bag, I found receipts, food wrappers, and a handful of pens. I turned the bag upside down and took my cell phone light to inspect all the dark crevices of the bag. Nothing incriminating. I moved on.

The next two bags I checked yielded similar results. There was ample evidence of all the work trips she had been on and the food she had eaten during her travels. However, there was nothing that even hinted at her affair with Matt.

But then, I checked her black backpack with gold trim. It must have had a dozen pockets, so it took time to diligently move through them all. In the front of the bag, there was a pocket inside of a pocket. In it, I could feel something hard. Unzipping the interior pocket, I could see the item as I pulled it out. It was a little ice hockey figurine wearing a Montreal Canadians jersey. It had a little loop on the end. It was either a Christmas tree ornament or a keychain figurine.

A level of furiousness came over me. There was only one person in Christy's life who had a love of the Montreal Canadians. Matt was born and raised in the Montreal area of Canada and was a diehard hockey fan. His kids all played hockey and he still played in an amateur league in New Jersey.

In fact, only two years earlier, Christy and I attended one of his games at a local ice rink along with a half dozen of her colleagues. It was a "playoff" game for their amateur league. I remember enjoying the experience when I attended the game. But now I just thought of it as a way for a lying and cheating, piece of shit dad to spend even more time away from his wife and kids. Reliving his glory days with a bunch of other middle-aged has-beens and having sex with a young, blonde employee in the apparent attempt to make himself feel young again were obviously where his priorities lied.

I put the figurine away and moved on from the bags in the closet to the drawers in her dresser. Starting with the bottom drawer, I worked my way up. The lower drawers contained nothing but clothes and some loose change. The upper drawers to the right contained much of the same. Just clothes and a few miscellaneous items that normally find their way into bedroom dressers. Then I opened the last drawer on the upper left of the bureau. At first glance there was nothing nefarious about it, just a few socks and some winter gloves. I dug down and felt a softcover book. It was the book I had found the night before titled, "I Love You, But I'm Not In Love With You." This time I decided to open it.

I flipped through the pages to see that Christy had made notes in the margins and underlined key phrases in the text. It seemingly was a book about falling out of love with someone that you have been with for a long time. It seemed to fit in with all the dramatic expressions of love we have come to know over the years as peddled by Hollywood and social media. The idea that true love is easy and effortless. The idea that when you find your "soul mate" you can ride off into the sunset together without a care in the world because you decided to cast aside normal, boring feelings love in exchange for the electricity and excitement of being "in love." (In the weeks to follow, I decided to read "Love Languages" by Gary Chapman, which vehemently disputes this notion of being perpetually "in love" as the basis for a lasting relationship.)

After reading all the highlighted text and handwritten notes that seemed to demonstrate that Christy was no longer "in love" with me, I placed the book back in the drawer. I started to wonder what else she had done to provide internal justification for her actions. I mean, everyone deserves happiness, right? She clearly thought she deserved happiness.

I do not fault her for that. We all want and feel deserving of happiness. I sure do. But what she seemed to be doing was using her own quest for happiness to justify destroying my life and the life we had built together. Her happiness was more important than the collateral damage of her actions on our family and friends. It was more important than destroying Matt's family of three wonderful children and a wife who gave up a career to take care of the kids so he could pursue his professional goals.

She deserved happiness, sure. But often, much of our happiness lies in the way we pursue it. I personally believe there are two types of happiness. One that is short-term because it is selfish and takes from those around you, and one that lasts a lifetime because it is selfless and breathes life and joy into others. Christy chose the former. If she had just told me that she did not feel the connection anymore and wanted to end our relationship, it would have been difficult, but it would have been the right and honorable thing to do.

But no. Instead she read books, listened to podcasts and took in any other source of information that could provide her with her own internal justification for betraying my trust and love. After all, her happiness was the most important thing to her, seemingly at any cost. Even if it was at the expense of our marriage. Even if it was at the expense of my happiness.

After I placed the book back where I had found it, I noticed something had shuffled in the drawer. It was a metallic wrapper that was about 5 inches long. Upon further inspection, I saw the words "Clear Blue." It had been opened with the white plastic base of an object sticking out. It was a pregnancy test. Before I removed the test from the wrapper, I noticed another one right below it in the drawer. To say my stomach twisted itself into a knot would be an incredible understatement. My stomach started doing somersaults as I pulled the first pregnancy test out of the wrapper.

"A blue horizontal line. What does that mean!?"

I quickly grabbed my phone to search what the indicator I found had meant. A moment of relief washed over me as the

Google results revealed that I was looking at a negative pregnancy test. However, that moment was fleeting. I still had to check the other test.

It too had a horizontal line, but also had the faintest of vertical lines crossing through it. The horizontal line was certainly more pronounced, but there was a nearly transparent vertical line and the two worked in concert to create a very faint cross shape. A check of the search results revealed that a pronounced blue cross indicated a positive pregnancy test. But what did a very, very faint vertical component of the cross mean?

I was panicking and sweating. Did this mean that this entire situation just absolutely hit the fan? Was Christy pregnant, on top of all of what was happening? I scoured the related search results on my phone. Incrementally, I felt a little better as the results noted that a faint vertical line also means the test is negative. I was not convinced on the first search, so I must have checked ten different websites. Finally, I put the tests back in the drawer and closed it.

"What else am I going to find?" I thought as I walked across the room towards her bedside table.

I know I had checked it the night before, but I had abandoned my search halfway through. I opened the top drawer and started to dig.

-19-

Devastation

The night before I had gone through the contents of her bedside table. It yielded a few notebooks, a bunch of old wrappers, numerous purchase receipts and the Christmas card stack which contained the "Iris" letter. I did not plan on spending much time looking through the bedside table again. But that is the thing about the initial days after discovering an affair. You are driven to an emotional state similar to a form of insanity. It did not matter how many times I checked a drawer or read a notebook. Each time I expected something different. Each time I figured I must have missed something on the previous search.

I started shoving things around the drawer to dig all the way to the bottom. There really was no organization to the contents. In fact, I found all the late-night snack used wrappers to be rather disgusting, and there were quite a few. Amongst the metallic linings of the various candy wrappers, I saw a certain one that looked eerily familiar with a white plastic piece sticking out. It was another pregnancy test in addition to the two tests I had found in her dresser. I took it out of the drawer and beneath it was yet another pregnancy test.

"What the hell is going on?" I thought.

The two negative tests in the dresser made some sense to me as perhaps she had been a little late at some point in the past and just wanted to confirm that she was not expecting. Before I found out about her affair, I actually would have been excited about having a baby. It would have been a surprise and certainly not planned, but being a father was always something I thought would come quite natural to me. I had a talent for making a child smile or laugh. I had a grown up in a house full of love, mixed in with the perfect amount of discipline by my amazing mom and dad. I had all the tools to be a loving and effective parent. It would have come at a time when my marriage to Christy was not perfect, but let's face it, how many peoples' lives or marriages are perfect when a baby arrives?

Finding these two additional tests immediately felt different though. The questions started flooding my mind. How often was she checking to see if she was pregnant? Was she just nervous about any delay in her period and just wanted some peace of mind? Why in the world was she saving these and who keeps four used pregnancy tests lying around?

I pulled out the white stick from the first wrapper. Similar to the tests I had found in the dresser, this too was marked by a single, solid horizontal line. Not Pregnant.

Then I inspected the second stick. I had barely pulled it out of its wrapping before I got the first glimpse at the result. The vertical blue line crossing the horizontal blue marking was not faint like the negative test in the bureau. Instead, it was pronounced, perhaps even more so than the horizontal line. There was no doubt about it. This pregnancy test was positive

For a split second, a wave of joy came over me. It must have been an innate reaction given that men are instinctually driven by a desire to procreate. I must have been unknowingly holding my breath while I checked the test. But with a deep exhale, my eyes began watering and the corners of my upper lip formed the slightest shape of a smile, while my jaw dropped and left my mouth to hang open. With elation I thought, "Oh my God, we are going to have a baby!"

But elation and happiness had no part in my life right now. The illusion of joy was tantalizing, yet fleeting and unreachable. It was like I was living in a dream world where love, joy and happiness were just out of my reach. I could see them as clear as day, but my arm was just too short to reach them and pull them into my grasp. The current reality of my life cascaded down on me, extinguishing any kindling of hope. My elation turned to panic.

"Shit, we are going to have a baby! What the hell do I do now?"

I placed the tests on top of the table and went into the kitchen to get a glass of water. My mouth and throat felt as dry as the desert baking in the midday sun. The lack of moisture produced the sensation of friction and scratchiness, inducing a vicious coughing fit. Each hack just made the problem worse as it felt as if my throat and lungs were wasting away and all I could do was expel the arid dust of their remains. I downed a full pint glass of water in less than five seconds. I quickly refilled it, then threw it back again. Most of the water went down my throat, but some remained on my lips and dripped down my chin. I did not care to wipe it away. I just leaned forward against the refrigerator with my forehead nestled into the nook of my right arm between the bicep and forearm. Tears joined the water that had dribbled down my chin. Diluted droplets of saline soon splattered on the floor beneath me.

With my left arm, I reached out to grasp a rocks glass from the bar cart adjacent to the refrigerator. I put it onto the counter to my right. Then I uncorked a bottle of small batch bourbon and began to pour. No ice, no water, no nothing. Just a rocks glass filled to the brim with bourbon, nearly a third of the bottle. I put it to my lips and let the amber liquid pour down my throat. In the span of three seconds I drank half the glass. My sensations had become so muted and foggy that the intense sting of the alcohol seemed to shock my system and remind me that I was alive.

I began to pace around the kitchen and continued to sip the remaining bourbon. I began to ponder some new questions. How long has she known? Why didn't she tell me? When could it have happened? How could it have happened? How does this affect how

I respond to the discovery of Christy's affair with Matt?

Ironically enough, there was one question I did not even think to ask myself.

"Was the baby even mine?"

I still was not internally sold on the fact that Christy had already been sleeping with Matt before the current work trip. For me, the only possible explanation for Christy's pregnancy was the result of our marital sex life. To think otherwise would have added a whole new level of devastation. I was adding a stiff dose of denial onto my insanity.

Finding the positive pregnancy test had temporarily suspended my search. But now I had another layer of mystery to unravel. In the same way I thought that I must have missed indications that Christy was having an affair, I also thought that there must be something in the condo that would have indicated that Christy was pregnant. I gulped down the remaining bourbon in the glass and refilled it before I resumed my search. I had a feeling it was going to be a long night.

After heading back into the bedroom, I rested the glass of bourbon on the bedside table next to the pregnancy tests that I had uncovered. I decided I was going to take a deep dive into the remaining contents of the bedside table, so I dropped down to the floor and pulled the drawers completely out of the wood frame. Some items had fallen behind the drawers and were resting on the bottom floor of the table once concealed by the recently removed bottom drawer. Included amongst these items was another moleskin notebook and a small box of condoms. It reminded me that back in October, Christy had been concerned that she had lapsed on switching out her birth control and needed to use a backup. Was this when it happened?

But that was over three months ago, which means that Christy would have taken the tests at least two months ago when she realized that she had missed her period. Why didn't she tell me?

You would think that she would have worked the news into one of my Christmas gifts or saved it for a New Year's surprise. If that is in fact when it happened, wouldn't she be showing early signs of the pregnancy at this point? Wouldn't I notice her dealing with bouts of nausea and morning sickness? At three months pregnant and entering her second trimester, wouldn't she start to be showing a slight bump?

I was puzzled. Either she was extremely skilled at concealing the physical signs of pregnancy or this was a more recent development. But the notion of a more recent development also seemed unlikely, as she had reinitiated her birth control and we had not had any sex in the last three months.

I dumped the contents of both the bottom and top drawers onto the floor into a heaping pile. There were wrappers, receipts, old Christmas cards, photos, outdated prescription medications, some magazines, random informational pamphlets and even a dried-out apple core which must have been there for quite some time. It was more representative of that random "junk" drawer that most people have in their kitchen than a bedside table. Between the receipts, wrappers and half-eaten apple, it easily could have been mistaken for a pile of trash.

In the mess of garbage on my bedroom floor, I noticed something familiar. It was the purple pamphlet with the flowing sketch of the outline of a woman's body with the title "*Meditation Guide.*" I had first seen it the night before and quickly moved past it. However, something was different upon further inspection. I noticed that I had misread the title during my quick glance at it the previous night. The pamphlet was not titled, "*Meditation Guide,*" but rather, "Medication Guide." Then underneath the sketch were two words that I had never heard of before.

"Mifepristone" and "Misoprostol."

Next to the pamphlet I saw one of the outdated prescription bottles. I picked it up and saw the word "Misoprostol" printed on the label. The date on the prescription indicated that the Christy had received the medication about two months earlier in December. Christy had not mentioned anything about starting a new medication regiment and the prescription bottle noted that it was one pill for a single use. It struck me as extremely odd that such a large prescription bottle was being used for a solitary dose of medicine.

The instructions for use were typed in small print under the drug's name. They indicated that Misoprostol should be taken within forty-eight hours of taking Mifepristone, or as directed by your doctor.

I then opened the pamphlet to discover the use of the medications. A discovery that would change my life and send waves of devastation crashing down on me.

Mifepristone is taken first to stop a pregnancy from growing. Misoprostol is then taken soon after to induce cramping and heavy bleeding to terminate the pregnancy.

Christy had an abortion.

There are no words for the level of despair and devastation that overtook me. I had been kneeling over the pile of the drawers' contents when I found the pamphlet and the prescriptions. Upon realizing what these items meant, my body just went numb. I felt like my upper body collapsed down on my lower body as if my bones had just suddenly given up all their strength to support me. My arms and legs seemed like they had lost all utility and were there to just dangle out of their sockets. My spine curled forward and slowly drifted to the right as it went limp like a wet noodle. All I could do was collapse into myself as I slowly rotated in a corkscrew like fashion until my body was laying contorted on the carpeted bedroom floor

I seemed to lose control of my faculties. The shock response was so powerful and there was nothing I could physically do to stop it. First, I started crying so intensely that it created incredibly painful muscle contractions deep in my diaphragm. I was temporarily blinded by my tears. The whaling noise I began to make started deep in my chest and rattled my throat before manifesting into a deafening, gargling moan. My mouth started watering with an intense amount of saliva, which slowly dribbled onto the floor each time I let out my horrific groan.

It was raw, animalistic and uncontrollable. Every few moans my body allowed itself a short window to get some air back into my lungs. As I sucked in as much air as I could, my saliva would also travel down my airway, inducing a violent, hacking cough. After the second or third breath, the hacking became so intense that I could feel my gastrointestinal system start to react. The master bathroom was directly behind where I was sprawled on the floor. With all my strength, I clamored to the bathroom and lifted the lid on the toilet. Feeling the stomach acid beginning to fill my esophagus, I gave into the unstoppable physical force that had taken over my body and vomited with the next round of groans.

The time to catch my breath between each groan was the only thing that stopped the upheaval of my stomach's contents. Then even when there was nothing left to expel, the motion kept going. The rolling muscle contractions from the depths of my intestines all the way up into my chest started to produce nothing more than a dry heave.

Seemingly, it was out of shear physical exhaustion that my body finally stopped reacting after a few agonizing minutes. I crawled back out into the bedroom as my mind started to shut down. Curled in the fetal position on the bedroom floor, I drifted into a lack of consciousness. However, I do not think I was asleep. It was more akin to physically being awake, but nothing existed in my mind. Broken and alone, I laid on the floor having learned that my wife ended the life of my child. A love never known. A joy never experienced. Potential that would never be realized because Christy decided to end the pregnancy, and I had no idea.

-20-

I Need to Call Her

It would be nearly thirty minutes before I would move from my lifeless position on the floor. The shock that had made me numb was ever so slightly being replaced by a feeling of restlessness. I climbed up from the floor and just started pacing back and forth across the condo. First, I walked to the entry door then through the kitchen and to the sliding glass door that leads to the balcony. Once I hit that checkpoint, I doubled back through the living area next to the kitchen and back to the entry door. Over a dozen times, I made the journey. Entry door then through the kitchen to the sliding glass door, then through the living area back to the entry door, then through the kitchen and to the sliding glass door, then through the living area and on and on.

With each lap, my restlessness grew. The rage inside me was like lighter fluid bubbling up until it was overflowing its container and pouring onto the fire that was lit underneath me. There was no way I could keep this in, I had to tell somebody.

Because she had been such a good friend the day before, and also because she was one of only two people in the entire world that knew about Christy's affair except for me, Christy and Matt, I dialed Monica's number on my cell phone.

Four even ringtones went by before I heard the receiver engage on the other end of the call.

"Hello," Monica answered.

"Hey Monica," I responded with a quivering voice.

I then paused and left a lingering silence in the conversation that was interrupted only by my deep labored breathing and audible sniffling. Monica waited as if she knew I needed a minute to gather myself.

She then asked, "Sean, what's going on? Are you okay?"

In a monotone and lifeless voice, I responded, "No, I'm really not okay Monica. I just found some stuff in Christy's bedside table. I found a positive pregnancy test, a few negative pregnancy tests and empty prescription bottles for a medication which terminates an early pregnancy. I think Christy had an abortion."

"Oh my God. Oh my God! Where are you now?" Her tone shifted to concern as she sought to quickly take stock of my mental and physical state.

"I'm in my bedroom just staring at the prescription bottles. I am at home. I found out less than an hour ago and didn't have anybody else to call." My response was as even and measured as I could make it as I tried to assure Monica that I was of sound body and mind.

She followed with some additional questions. "When did it happen? How did you find out? Are you sure it's –"

She seemed to cut herself off before she asked the question of whether I was the father.

I responded to her questions, "I was going through her bedside table because I knew there just had to be something I missed. I just had a feeling she could not have possibly hid this so well from me. I thought I would find a love letter, a card, a photo, something. But not this, I had no idea I would find this. I do not even know her anymore. How could the woman I fell in love with be capable of this?"

I continued. "The prescription is from last December. I noticed that Christy was being a little more withdrawn and I also noticed that she seemed to have her period for an abnormally long amount of time. It was even to the point where I was concerned and asked if she needed to see a doctor. But she shrugged it off and just said that 'it was just a little longer and heavier this time for some reason'."

I started to immediately recount the timeline of events from the day of the prescription's date in my mind. For some reason, I could remember that day because it was somewhat unusual. I had a field meeting in the morning that required me to take our SUV out to the jobsite. I typically walk to work, so it is unusual that I drive except for work meetings such as this. After my meeting I intended to drop the car back off at the condo before I started my fifteen-minute walk to the office. This way, I would avoid paying to park the car downtown and I could pop up to see Christy for a few minutes during the middle of the day. Perhaps we could even have lunch.

When I informed Christy of my plan that day, she responded with seemingly sincere appreciation. However, she noted that she had been working from home so much over the past few months that she was thinking about a change of scenery for the day. Perhaps a local coffee shop or café. I encouraged her to take advantage of that idea as I thought it would be good for her. She had been so stressed about "work" lately.

When I arrived back from dropping the car off at the condo, I noticed that our other car was missing too. Nothing nefarious crossed my mind. I just thought to myself that she had perhaps decided to try a spot in a different neighborhood that was a bit too far to walk with her laptop and work bag.

I texted Christy a little bit later that afternoon that I was thinking that I would walk straight to the grocery store to pick up a few things and asked her to send me a list of anything she could think of. Around 4:30 that afternoon she sent me a list of about ten items and ended her message with "Thanks so much for picking these up babe! I love you!" Everything seemed normal, as if it were just another day in Christy's life. How did she do it?

Then I thought about the weekend before the date on the prescription bottle. Christy and I had hosted two of my cousins who came out to visit Denver because one of them was considering relocating to the city at the time. It was a joyous weekend with our visitors. Dinners out, excursions around the state, and plenty of brewery and cocktail bar visits. Christy had been drinking with the rest of us that weekend as if pregnancy were not even in the farthest reaches of her mind. Did she know then that she was pregnant? How could she not if she probably had missed two of her periods at this point? Did she know she was going to get an abortion anyway, so she thought, "Fuck it, I'll have another drink?"

I relayed this story of the chain of events leading up to and including that December day to Monica. She silently listened and then softly said, "Sean, I know you were waiting for her to come back this weekend to confront her. But I think you need to call her. This is too much. There is just no way you can carry this for the next five days all alone. You need to call her."

Monica was right. I had to call Christy. I kept repeating that fact to Monica as if I were trying to convince her, but really, I was attempting to convince myself.

"I need to call her. I need to call her. I need to call her."

I knew I would have to confront Christy at some point, but I had convinced myself that I still had time. That the confrontation was all the way at the end of the week, and it was only Monday. However, the truth became apparent to me. I did not want to confront her for a whole host of reasons, but primarily because I was living in the comfort of a bubble. A sad and painful bubble, but a bubble, nonetheless.

Right now, I could control the narrative of what Christy had done in my own thoughts. I could package it, rectify it and process it in a way that was at least digestible and palatable to me. However, once I introduced Christy into the dialogue, she would have a say in the narrative. With one quick retort, she could burst my bubble with the prick of reality. Right now, I could justify the entire scenario in the context that I wanted.

I had the power of complete control over the narrative. I dreaded relinquishing some of that power to Christy, particularly since she was armed with the truth and facts of what she had done. All I had was speculation, two text messages, some pregnancy tests and prescription bottles for an early abortion medication regiment.

I thanked Monica for being such a good friend and told her that I would call Christy. I hung up the phone and took a deep breath along with one more look at the evidence I had gathered. I am not sure why, but I pulled up the screenshot I had taken of the messages on Christy's phone a few days earlier. Before I called Christy, I read and reread the crucial message about twenty times in order to memorize it. Feeling sufficiently prepared, or at least as prepared as I could be, I pulled up Christy's contact card on my phone and hit the green phone icon.

The phone began to ring. Then it rang a few more times and continued for about thirty seconds. Finally, the ringing stopped and transitioned to a prerecorded message.

"Hi, this is Christy. I'm so sorry I missed your call, but if you could leave your name, number and a brief message, I will get back to you as soon as I can."

Before the customary "beep" occurred that signals for the caller to start recording his message, I had disconnected the phone and began to call again. Over thirty seconds of ringing follow, along with the same prerecorded message.

When Christy called the day before as she was driving to the Florida resort where her company's meetings were being held, she mentioned that Tuesday would be one of the busiest days and that the team would likely be strategizing late into Monday night before the big day. Thoughts swirled through my head about what "strategizing late into the night" actually meant. Was she sincere, or was that just her way of saying, "Please don't bother me while I am fucking the man I actually want to be with?"

After the two failed phone call attempts, I decided to send a few text messages to Christy which indicated the seriousness with which I was trying to reach her.

I typed, "I don't care what you are doing, or who you are doing it with. You need to call me RIGHT NOW!!!"

I then followed up with a statement of the relentlessness in which I would attempt to reach her.

"I WILL NOT stop calling until we talk."

I then attempted to call two more times. My third attempt went through the typical thirty seconds before her voicemail message initiated. However, on the fourth attempt, a call came through a split second before my outgoing call connected to her phone. It was Christy. She was attempting to call me back.

I accepted the call.

-21-

The Call

"Hello," I spoke into the mouthpiece.

Christy responded, "Hey Sean. Is everything okay? Sorry I missed your calls; I was in the meeting I had told you about. What's the matter, Is this an emergency?"

It struck me how calm and matter of fact she seemed. Even to this day, I think about her calm and measured tone. My repeated calls and cryptic messages must have communicated that something was wrong. In the same way I will never understand how she was able to compartmentalize her thoughts and emotions to carry on a relationship with Matt while she was married to me, I will never quite understand the still and calm in her voice at the beginning of this phone call.

With tears flooding back into my eyes I simply asked, "How could you?"

Christy seemed relatively unphased by the question and responded in a repeating fashion, "How could I? What are you talking about?"

"I know." I responded back.

"What are you talking about?" She asked defiantly.

I simply repeated the same statement. "I know."

"Sean, you know what?" She asked with exasperation.

My succinct statements of the fact that I knew about her affair almost seemed to annoy her, given the tone in which she asked this last question.

This time I responded forcefully, "Christy, I fucking know! I know about you and Matt. I know you are having an affair. Do you deny it?"

I decided to cut out the nuance and forcefully tell her that I knew she was cheating on me. Maybe it was a nervous reaction on her part, but her response almost seemed to be accompanied by a condescending chuckle.

"Sean, I really do not know what you are talking about and don't know where you are getting this from. Matt is nothing more than a mentor and a friend. Why are you..."

I cut her off before she could continue her hollow defense strategy of deflecting and answering all my statements and questions with questions of her own. I decided to simply state the evidence in a matter of fact way as if I was a stenographer reading back a court transcript with all the emotion removed. From memory, I recited the text message that Matt had sent to Christy.

"So close. Only 1 more night to go. I'm out of my mind excited to see you. I keep thinking about being together and cannot contain myself anymore. You are the woman I want to take care of, touch, feel and be with and tomorrow I get to let all those feelings out with you - don't worry, I'll wait until after the SB for some of them. I've missed you so much sweetheart. I love you."

I then finished off my monotone reading of Matt's text message by noting, "Then six winking smiley faces at the end."

I followed up by asking the question again. "Do you deny it?"

On the other end of the call I heard an audible sigh from Christy followed by an extended pause. I was not going to speak again until I got an answer to my question.

After a few awkward and agonizing seconds, Christy simply responded "No, I don't deny it."

Up until that moment, my case was built on speculation supported by evidence I had found by investigating Christy's personal items. This investigation was based solely on my suspicions, which were the direct result of her recent actions. Even given what I had found, I still felt a certain level of guilt and madness that I had stooped to a level where I invaded her privacy, which in turn led me to reach an unconfirmed conclusion that Christy was having an affair.

I almost felt a sense of relief that my gut instincts were in fact accurate. It was right of me to think that Christy was acting suspicious because her actions themselves were nefarious and worthy of suspicion. Christy had made her statement of confession that she was indeed cheating on me with Matt. She then attempted to explain her actions.

"I never meant for it to happen. I've been so stressed, and you haven't been there for me. I don't even think you need me (an expression of unhealthy codependency). You never seem to care…"

Again, I cut her off. I have always tended to err on the side of nonconfrontation. But hearing Christy respond to the revelation that I had discovered her affair by throwing accusatory "you" statements back at me seemed to blow the gasket on the tank that held my bellicose reserves locked away. Forcefully speaking into the phone, I took back control of the conversation.

"No! You don't get to fucking talk! You are just going to shut up and listen!"

I then proceeded to explain everything about the weekend before she left for Florida. I explained in detail the agony of discovering Matt's text messages on her phone. I described in painful detail how I put on a brave face to have one more day of normal before she left. I recounted my experience during the watch party the night before, dreading the end of the game because that was when Matt was going to supposedly "let his feelings out with her." I noted how she thought she was so smooth sending me a text towards the end of the game that both stated that she was heading to bed and that she was too exhausted to talk.

What she did not realize is that I knew exactly where she was going. She was going to be reunited with her fifty-year-old fantasy man so she could selfishly have sex with him behind my back. She thought I was blissfully ignorant and aloof of what she was doing.

I then pivoted to my thoughts on her feelings for Matt.

"I can't believe I ever thought that guy was worth a damn. He isn't worthy of being a piece of shit stuck on the bottom of my shoe. He claims to love you. Do you love him? I can't believe you do. I can't believe you could ever have feelings for a fucking piece of shit that would sleep with a subordinate, betraying the trust of not only his wife of almost twenty years, but the trust of his three innocent kids. Did either of you even think of them? Did either of you even think of me? How fucking selfish are you!?"

I did not really expect an answer to the questions I was asking. They really were not even questions, but more like statements in the form of questions. I was on a roll with communicating to Christy exactly how I felt about her so-called feelings for Matt. It was akin to a parent lecturing his child after she had done something wrong. The questions were not meant to be answered, at least not right then in the moment. Instead, the intent of the questions was meant to cause Christy guilt. It was meant to make her contemplate the damage she had done through her selfish acts.

That may sound vindictive and calculating, I know. However, it was one of the first times since I had discovered Christy's affair that I felt like I had some semblance of control. Control of my actions. Control of my emotions. Control of the conversation. It was an extremely important moment in surviving those first days.

For one of the first times in my life, the words poured out of me rather than being caught on the tip of my tongue while my mind weighed the ramifications of saying them. It came from an overwhelming sense that there was nothing that could ever justify her actions. I believed I was sincerely right in admonishing her actions, and she was completely wrong for having committed infidelity.

Christy managed to squeeze a few words in response to my litany of questions and admonitions.

"I didn't mean for it to happen, but I do have feelings for him."

I quickly seized on her statement and launched right back into an anger fueled monologue.

"You didn't mean for it to happen? What the hell is that supposed to mean? I'm sorry, but it is a pretty huge leap from having feelings for someone to having sex with them, particularly when you both are in committed marriages and have the prospect of destroying your families on the line. No! You knew exactly what you were doing, and you didn't give a shit about me or anybody else."

I continued. "It's because your happiness is paramount, right? Screw everything else as long as Christy is happy. Is that what you learned from all the bullshit books you've been reading about finding your happiness? Is that really their intent? For a wife to find happiness by stabbing her loyal partner, who has stood by her side since the age of sixteen, in the back? Is that what those books taught you? Happiness lies in lying to, and cheating on, the person who loves you?"

I then started to describe what I had found while going through her personal items.

"I went through all of your things Christy. I saw your book called 'I Love You, but I'm Not In Love With You.' Didn't that book at least prompt you to be honest with me about how you were feeling? Nobody deserves this. I did nothing to deserve this. I have been a good and loyal husband to you. But you don't even have the decency or shred of respect for me to voice your considerations for leaving the marriage. Instead, you live a double life behind my back with Matt, your fucking boss' boss. What is wrong with you?"

I could feel myself getting emotional and starting to hyperventilate. My heart was beating out of my chest as I uttered the hardest words of the conversation.

"And you were pregnant? I found the tests. I also found the abortion medications. Misoprostol and Mifepristone. You had an abortion?"

I could not hear a response on the other end of the line, but I could sense Christy's reaction through the phone. Her silence seemed to indicate that my question hit an emotional nerve deep within her. Maybe it was her way of managing her emotions around everything I was saying, but her tone became rigid and stoic.

"Yes." She simply stated.

I was not so stoic and rigid.

"Who are you?" I responded in a breathy and quivering voice.

It was a question of disbelief that the person I married could be capable of having an affair, getting pregnant and having an abortion, all behind my back. These discoveries made me feel as if my well-being, my love and even my life were deemed worthless by my own wife. I had to let that sentiment sink in for a moment. I was deemed worthless by my own wife.

In her decision making, she had decided that it was more important to end the life of an innocent unborn child than to disclose the truth to her husband. A lot of the specific words of our vows went through my head in those initial days. However, the most prominent were "I promise to be true to you." I think wedding vows generally start with that phrase for a distinct reason. A marriage, or any serious and meaningful relationship, can only survive in truth. Everything that follows that statement in the wedding vows is an offshoot of being true to your partner, and frankly meaningless, if truth is not present.

I still could not fathom contemplating anything other than the notion that the baby belonged to me. I responded to her answer in kind.

"How could you? Why did you do this?"

I collapsed to the ground of the bedroom in a similar fashion to when I had found the pamphlet and pregnancy termination prescription bottles.

I continued, "Did I not have a say in the life of our child? You had no right to do this. That was our baby! That was my baby! You had no fucking right to kill my baby!"

I wish I could convey the emotion and desperation I felt in those statements. There simply are no words to describe such a depressed human state. I thought I had been robbed of being a father by my ex-wife. A level of desperation and instinctual sadness kicked in stronger than I have ever felt in my life. Without thinking rationally about it in hindsight, but just putting myself back in that moment, if I could have traded my life for that child's, I would have.

"It wasn't yours." Christy responded.

"What do you mean? How do you know it wasn't mine?

Christy then attempted to lay out the timeline of events as to why the child could not have been mine. But I also started doing the mental math.

Christy had taken the prescription abortion pills in December. Those pills are generally only used for terminating a pregnancy up to ten weeks from conception. Ten weeks before the day she took them in December would have been sometime in late September or early October. It struck me that Christy and I had not had sex since before our wedding anniversary in mid-September. I remembered this specifically, because it was so striking to me that on our wedding anniversary, any attempts at romance and intimacy were shot down. I even planned a weekend away in Boulder, Colorado full of romantic restaurants, walks through the local shops, and a stay in a fancy hotel suite in an attempt to jump start some form of passion in our marriage. These efforts were met with rejection.

So, if it were not me, when could Matt have impregnated Christy?

I scoured my memory of Christy's work trips. The only one that fit the timeline was a work retreat that Christy had participated in at a resort in northern New Jersey in late October. That was the only time she was back in New Jersey and in Matt's company without me present for a portion of the trip. The only other time in which Christy visited New Jersey before her abortion was during Thanksgiving. On that trip, I accompanied her, and we stayed at her parent's house the entire time.

I zeroed on that specific week at the end of October.

I had decided to book a flight to New Jersey to visit family that coincided with the end of Christy's work trip. We had done this many times over the previous months and years as a way to coordinate our visits home from Denver to coincide with her work travel. Christy's company was located only forty-five minutes away from both of our parent's homes, so I would generally fly in on Thursday or Friday at the end of the work week and we would spend the weekend with our loved ones before flying back together on Sunday.

That particular trip stood out to me because it was the weekend of my mother's birthday. I had only decided about a week in advance to fly in as a surprise for her. I landed at Newark airport at just after midnight on Friday morning. Christy happened to be staying at a hotel near her office in northern New Jersey, which just so happened to be the same hotel where we had held our wedding reception a little over seven years earlier. It crossed my mind that we would be staying in the same hotel as our wedding night for only the second time since we had been married. Another opportunity to infuse some passion back into our relationship, at least I thought.

When I arrived at the hotel around one in the morning, Christy barely awakened to greet me before falling back asleep. This was pretty much par for the course at the time, so I did not think much of it besides a slight amount of disappointment. I settled in and fell asleep.

Thinking about this timeline, it struck me that Christy had stayed in that hotel for several nights that week. I became sick with the thought that I had slept in the bed where Matt had sex with Christy. Obviously, I had no idea at the time, but the thought was revolting to me.

"Did I sleep in the bed where you and Matt conceived a child?" I asked with disgust.

I continued before she could respond. "Did he not wear a condom? What happened to your birth control?"

"It just happened." She responded.

I quickly fired back, "So, you let him finish inside you then?"

The details mattered to me. I needed her to acknowledge the specifics of exactly how she ended up pregnant with Matt's baby.

"No, it wasn't like that," she responded. "It just happened."

Did she take me for any idiot? The floodgates were open now. Did she think that sparing the details that Matt's semen ended up inside her vagina would provide some sort of solace for me? Like just about every other person in America, I went to Sex Ed. I am quite sure I know how these things happen!

Her dodging and deflection of the facts were fueling an anger deep inside. I decided to inject the facts right back into the conversation.

"No, the truth is that you were reckless and had an affair with Matt. Because of your recklessness, you ended up getting pregnant with his child. It must have been the weekend of my Mom's birthday, right? Did it happen at our hotel? Did I sleep in that same bed? How could you Christy? I don't even know who you are anymore. The Christy I married would have never cheated on me. The Christy I married would have never had an abortion. At the end of it, you decided to lie to me and to kill an innocent baby behind my back. Why didn't I have a say? Are you really that much of a coward that you couldn't tell me? Did you hide it from Matt, or did he know? If he did know, what kind of shithole of a man stands by as this happens? You killed that baby because of nothing more than it was an inconvenience! That is a fucking fact!"

This is not meant to be a commentary on the debate over the topic of abortion, but rather a recounting of my personal experience dealing with fact that my ex-wife had an abortion without my knowledge and the personal impact that her decision has had on me. Even though I had no idea at the time, I feel as if I ultimately played a major role in her decision. The inconvenience of telling me provided enough reason to end a child's life. There is no getting around that issue.

Fast-forward six months and what would have been different? I discovered everything, Christy and I were heading for divorce, and families and futures were ruined. Those outcomes would have been exactly the same if she had told me while she was pregnant. The only difference is that a baby would be alive today if not for her cowardice and selfishness.

Living with these facts is a reality that I still struggle with to this day. Being an unknowing third party in the death of a potential life is an abhorrent reality of my life. It is a reality I would have never chosen. But I was not given the opportunity to have a say. I found out about Christy's abortion nearly two months after it had happened. I was powerless to have any direct effect on that decision, but she had already sealed my fate in forever being indirectly involved in her decision. She and Matt determined that ending a baby's life was more convenient than allowing me to know the truth.

Between Matt and Christy, they make hundreds of thousands of dollars a year in HUMAN RESOURCES! This was not a case of inability to raise a child or a case of pregnancy by some abusive form. This was a case of two people who were apparently "in love" who decided to end a life because the alternative was the embarrassment and inconvenience of telling me the truth. There is no moral ambiguity for me on this subject. To them, avoiding inconvenience and continuing their deception were more important than a baby's life.

A consistent theme of my call with Christy was the repeated question, "Who are you?"

I asked it over and over. It came from such a deep sense of disbelief. Was it disbelief that she was capable of such awful things or that she was so capable of looking me in the eyes everyday as she did them? It did not really matter which question was more of the source of my disbelief. I truly could not comprehend either. These were questions that I never thought I would have to ask myself about Christy.

I was overwhelmed by the feeling that this is not the woman I had married. But that was followed up quickly with a personal sentiment that I had been played for a fool. I should have been able to see this right in front of me, no matter how much Christy relied on my trust to hide right in plain sight. It seemed like Christy and Matt, who up until a few days ago I considered a friend, had completely disregarded the impact their affair would have on me. So, I decided to continue the conversation with an appeal to the consideration of Matt's wife and kids.

"What about Linda and those kids? Did you even think about them? Linda gave up her career to be a dutiful and loyal wife. What is she supposed to do now? What are her kids supposed to do? Do you understand the gravity of what you have done? You have destroyed my life, but do you realize that you have destroyed Linda's marriage to Matt? Do you realize that you have obliterated the relationship that Matt's kids will have with their father? What am I supposed to do now Christy? Linda deserves to know that her husband is a lying, cheating asshole. Does she not?

Christy then cut me off.

"Linda already knows."

"What do you mean she already knows?" I retorted.

"She found out a little while ago. She and Matt separated after she found out," Christy explained.

I asked, "How long has Linda known?"

"What does that matter?" Christy asked with exhaustion in her voice.

So, I asked again more forcefully.

"How long has Linda known!?"

With an audible exhale, Christy stated, "She has known since last summer."

"Last summer as in this past year?" I inquired.

Christy replied, "No. She found out in the summer of 2017."

Up until that point, the timeline I had built in my head only allowed me to think of Christy's affair as a recent development. It was a foolish benefit of the doubt that I continued to give my wife, considering what she had done and was still doing to me.

Immediately after I found the text messages from Matt a few days earlier, I had convinced myself that there may have still been a chance to stop the physical culmination of their affair. Then my conversation with Monica on Sunday revealed that it was likely that the affair had been going on for some time based on Matt's overtly explicit and affectionate language in describing his excitement to see Christy. Finally, the discovery of Christy's abortion of the baby she had apparently conceived with Matt, indicated that the affair dated back to at least October of 2018.

But the summer of 2017? That was over a year and a half ago! Christy had been cheating on me for at least a year and a half, if not longer, as that is just when Matt's wife, Linda, found out. I felt deflated and I could not stand Christy's voice on the other end of the line for another second.

"That's it, I'm done with this shit. I can't talk to you anymore."

To the outsider, my statement was strong and authoritative. However, on the inside I was feeble, exhausted and weak.

"Okay." Christy responded. "Are you going to physically be okay? When can I talk to you again to make sure you are okay?"

I snapped back, "Oh, now you give a shit about my wellbeing? Why didn't you care about it while you were on your back, underneath Matt?"

I continued, "I will talk to you when I am good and ready to talk to you."

With that, I hung up on Christy.

-22-

This Thing They Call a Panic Attack

I could not tell if I was more red hot with anger or weighed down by sorrow. But whatever it was, after I ended the call with Christy, I was simply tired. My voice was nearly hoarse from talking almost uninterrupted for the last forty-five minutes. I am usually a reserved person, but Christy's initial denials of the truth, which required me to read the damning text messages back to her, unleashed a roaring response that I could not seem to control. It was as if the events of the past few days had created thousands of individual little cracks in a dam. But it was not until Christy hit that network of cracks with a hammer, did the bottled-up thoughts and emotions come pouring out with overwhelming force.

I do not think I had ever spoken to Christy with such power and anger before. Throughout our marriage, I had always checked my words and my tone to be more reserved in deference to her feelings and emotions. Perhaps I should have been more direct along the way. Perhaps I should have been more willing to speak honestly despite her feelings along the way. These are lessons I carry forward with me. There were a lot of opportunities for honest conversations during both our premarital relationship and our marriage. But both Christy and I avoided them because we are both non-confrontational people. Perhaps confrontation in small, manageable, and productive doses along the way is healthy for a marriage or relationship.

I decided to call one of my brothers. The call with Christy had made me quickly realize that I needed someone I loved in the trenches with me. I told him everything. I told him about the affair, about the abortion, and what I knew about the timeline. He listened intently and mostly was silent. I am not sure if it was because he was shocked by the news, did not know what to say, or was just plain angry as hell. Possibly it was a combination of all three. He offered to come see me as soon as he could. I declined and noted that Christy would be back at the end of the week. It would have been great to have my brother around for support, but I needed to face Christy alone when the time came. He assured me repeatedly that he loved me, that he and the rest of the family were firmly behind me, and that he was so sorry for what Christy had done to me.

I thanked my brother and hung up the phone. Then something unexpected happened. I immediately regretted disclosing to him what had happened. Looking back now, it was a ridiculous feeling to have because I do not know what I would have done if I had not told my brother about what happened. I needed to tell him, and I am so glad I did. But in that moment, I felt like I had just introduced a risk to my process of deciding what to do about Christy's affair. Those initial days and weeks were an agonizingly brutal mental game of balancing risk and support.

My brother's reassuring words provided a level of support that I desperately needed. However, telling my brother introduced several theoretical causalities of unintended consequences to a number of hypothetical conclusions. What if my brother accidentally shared my situation with my family before I was ready? What if I eventually wanted to reconcile my relationship with Christy but my family was aware of what she did, and I would have to choose between her or my family. What if I did choose Christy, but ultimately that choice made me resent her? If I ended up resenting her, would we just get divorced anyway even if we did reconcile in the short term? Would that scenario leave me lonelier than I already felt, having lost my wife and alienating my family?

I almost wanted to immediately go and take back the information I had shared with my brother. But the cat was out of the bag as they say. In fact, the bag had an entire zoo in there and the animals were chaotically running loose all around me. I could not seem to latch on to one feeling about what had just transpired in my conversation with Christy.

Being an engineer and a bit of a space geek, I love the movie, "The Martian" with Matt Damon. At a point in that movie, he speaks to survival in space as a series of problems to be solved in a certain succession. He says you identify one problem and you get to work. You solve that problem. Then you move on to the next and the next and the next after that. That if you solve enough problems you get to survive.

But what do you do when all the problems hit you at one time? How do you triage your thoughts? How do you command your mind to focus while it is getting bombarded? That is the dilemma I faced.

The first problem I faced was starting to think about coping with the fact that the baby was not mine. But how did I know it was not mine? All I had was Christy's word and my hazy recollection of our sex life over three months prior. How could I know for sure? The baby had been gone for over two months so there was no way to prove that the child was not mine, right? I started to wrestle with the fact that I will never know for certain that the child was not mine. It may be highly unlikely that it was mine, but I can never be 100% certain.

But as soon as I started to wrap my mind around tackling the uncertainty of a paternal connection to the pregnancy Christy terminated, the thought about Matt's wife's knowledge of the affair a year and a half ago drifted into my mind. Why didn't she tell me over a year ago when she found out? Before I had spoken to Christy, I was agonizing over the thought that disclosing my discovery to Linda would lead to the destruction of Matt's kids' relationship with their father. Linda certainly deserved to know the truth that her husband of almost twenty years is nothing more than a lying cheat who found a younger model. But that truth would surely be a catalyst for the most devastating moment of both her and her kids' lives. So many of my thoughts were with protecting Matt's family because he was not. Why did no one think that I deserved the same consideration? The music apparently stopped over a year and a half ago and I was the only schmuck who was still waiting for a chair.

Then I thought about what Christy was doing right then and there, after I hung up on her. I sincerely wondered if the call had any effect on what she thought of her actions with Matt. Had I ruined the rest of her romantic trip with Matt? I really hope I was effective in throwing water on the fires of their apparent passion for each other. But what if the call had the opposite effect? What if her first reaction was to run to Matt, realizing that everything would change after this trip? Would they just use the remaining time they had together to explore the true depths of their passion? I mean, what did they have to lose?

If I had driven her deeper into Matt's arms, did it really matter at this point? This was a man who looked me straight in the eye as we had an in depth one on one conversation at a wedding for one of Christy's coworker's in May of 2018 while he was sleeping with my wife. This was a man who abandoned his family. This is a man who impregnated my wife and then stood by as she terminated her pregnancy. What could they do now that would be any worse than what they had already done to me?

Then my thoughts went to the impact on Christy's family. Then the impact on my family. How would I tell my friends? Did I want to tell any more of my friends or family yet? If I did tell any of my family and friends, would there even be an option to save my marriage? Would there be increasing pressure to give up on my relationship with Christy which had been a staple of my life ever since I was a teenager? Did I really want my situation reduced to tired clichés like, "Once a cheater, always a cheater" or, "She's not sorry she cheated, she's just sorry she got caught."

These questions and thoughts were just the tip of the iceberg of what was swirling around my head. I tried to pick just one thought and focus on it. But the sheer number of them was just too great for my mind to handle. They were like a virus. Thoughts in small numbers can be managed, mentally filed away and systematically solved. Like Matt Damon said, "you solve one problem and then you solve the next problem." If I solved enough problems, I could surely get my sanity and peace of mind back.

But what if all the problems hit in such a large volume that they simply overwhelmed my system and ability to manage them? The mere act of isolating a thought in an effort to solve it created a problem in its own right. In the time it took for me to process a single thought, five more had flooded in. I did not know how to process this sensation at the time, because I had honestly never experienced anything quite like it in my life.

The impossibly overwhelming flood of information rendered me helpless and rudderless. I could not control it and I was powerless in the face of it. My heart started racing. The pace of my breathing increased. A pressure started building in my chest. The pressure was light at first, but it increased and increased until my rapid breathing turned into hyperventilating to counteract the force of the pressure. My eyes started tearing and my body started rocking back and forth

For the first time that I can remember in my life, I was having a legitimate and diagnosable panic attack. Utterly helpless to its power, I just sat down and let it envelope me. That was all I could think to do about the panic attack.

It's like a rising tide in the caverns of my mind. The way out is hard to find. I'm gasping for air. This fear has taken

me. The water is getting deep. There's only lonely when gasping for air.

I started my story with these lyrics of a song I wrote nearly nine months after I experienced the fear and panic of the unrelenting anxiety that Christy's betrayal introduced into my life. It took nine months to write about the experience. It took nine months for me to be able to understand what I was feeling in those initial days, process those feelings and then articulate the feelings. Even then, words were not enough. I had to give those words additional context and emotion. I had to give those words a rhythmic melody with a minor tonality.

If you are reading this and experiencing the wretched and helpless feeling of anxiety and panic, I hope the words of my story or any other book on anxiety or fear will help. Anxiety and panic are evil and overwhelming feelings. When severe enough, you cannot just simply snap out of it, as some people like to think that you should be able to. Then, you add the internal pressure, as well as the external social pressure this sentiment brings, which only throws more fuel on the fire.

I discovered, feelings of anxiety, panic, and fear have an eerie relationship to the feeling of love in that they are an antithesis of each other, but their mutual existence dwells in a departure from what is considered to be rational thought. Yet, as humans we try to rationalize these feelings with words, poems and songs. But the truth is, we do not truly take control of any of these irrational feelings, until we allow ourselves to embrace their irrational existence. You cannot describe these feelings or thoughts and put them into a calculation or formula. They simply just exist. In the case of love, it is a beautiful, irrational existence that brings unbelievable joy to our lives. In the case of anxiety, it can consume us and lead to devastating and horrible repercussions.

Just as the "fool in love," does not regain control over his life until he accepts that the love he has is an unexplainable force in his life, a man in the grips of crippling fear and anxiety does not regain power over his panic until he accepts the same. My inability to gather my thoughts in a constructive and coherent way started leaving each one of those thoughts in a vacuum of sorts. Left in this vacuum, our natural tendency is to project our most negative responses onto these thoughts. The only thing that can loosen the tightening grip of panic is to start getting busy. Just sitting there, letting my panic drown me, was not going to help.

My problem was that I had so many questions swirling around my head and each of these questions was complex, requiring deep thought and consideration. To add to the pressure, each of these questions also had the potential to lead to an answer containing a hard truth that would fundamentally alter the course of my life. I decided to seek refuge in my affinity for the analytical process. I needed to think critically. But not about any one of the individual questions flooding my mind, the time for that would come later. No, my first step was to solve the problem of the immense volume of questions itself and how I could capture each of these questions for future analysis.

So how do I capture all these fleeting thoughts and questions individually before they fall into the rabbit holes which descend to the depths of my mind? Well I did something that I have not done since I was a child. I wrote.

It was honestly surprising for me as I have never been an avid writer. In fact, the idea of keeping a diary always seemed a bit cheesy to me. But I was desperate, and I needed to do something actionable. So, I pulled out a blank Moleskine notebook and started on the first page.

The first thing I did was put the date at the top of the page. February 4, 2019. For some reason it felt important to keep an accurate account of the timeline of my writing. I had a feeling that I would not only want to keep a record of my thoughts, but also the timing of those thoughts. This proved invaluable as I moved through the coming days and weeks, as I had a date stamped reference for what I felt and when I felt it. The journals I kept would resemble a man of madness to the outside reader devoid of context. When I reread these journals, it was remarkable to see the cyclical nature of my feelings.

Questions led to anger. Anger led to rejection. Rejection led to acceptance. Acceptance led to hope. Hope led to action. Action led to conflict. Conflict led to questions. Questions led to anger, and on and on and on. This cyclical pattern was my existence for almost three months straight after I found out about Christy's affair.

The cycle all started for the first time that night. As painful as it was to be stuck in this manic loop, I am grateful for it. Because that seemingly manic loop was actually the product of processing my thoughts. By writing down the questions that were swirling around in my head I accomplished three things.

First, it allowed me to document and archive them before they were momentarily lost to the raging storm in my mind. Notice I said they were momentarily lost, not totally lost. Just like lighting in a thunderstorm, they would flash out of nowhere and then vanish as quickly as they appeared. You know it is going to strike again, but you do not know when. I was perpetually in this storm and I was not going to be able to get out until I could capture every thought on paper like catching lighting in a bottle.

Second, writing my thoughts and questions down allowed me to triage them. I was able to go back and assign them priority. I was able to organize them in a way that made sense. There was no sense diving deep into the question of "How did I know the baby was not mine?" before I answered the question of "What is the actual timeline of Christy's affair and when did Matt and Christy start having unprotected sex?"

Finally, seeing these thoughts and questions on paper gave me a sense of control over them. Even though the Moleskine notebook was nothing more than an inanimate object, the pages took on a personality when I wrote my feelings on them. It was like having a friend who was being brutally honest with me. Those pages did not sugar coat anything. Those pages listened to every word I said and then recited it back to me in the exact words I had written. Those pages did not seek to make me feel better or worse, rather they simply sought to show me the ugly truth of what was in my head. In truth, there is power; and in power there is control.

I would have many more panic attacks over the coming days, weeks and months. I could not control when or how they would come for me and envelope me in their miserable net. However, I did learn a valuable lesson that night. Panic is when loss of control joins forces with hopelessness. The two feed off each other and together they grow like a cancer. To quell the panic, you either must restore hope or regain control. I will be honest; I had no hope in those initial days.

Hope involves seeing the forest through the trees and establishing a direction towards open pastures. For me, the first days of survival were marked by the trees creating a prison for me. There was no direction that would provide hope, at least not yet. So, my only option was control. I may have been cornered and caged in by hopelessness and fear, but if I could harness my thoughts, I could gain control over them and stave off the panic for one more night.

-23-

Taking Back Control

I stayed awake journaling until nearly two o'clock in the morning so I knew I would not be getting much sleep again that night. However, when I did finally fall asleep, I slept the best I had in days. Writing had allowed my mind to temporarily calm down enough to drift into a peaceful slumber. I did not even remember getting into bed or my head settling into the pillow. All I recall is entering a vacuum of time and cognition, followed by the melodic ringtone of the alarm on my phone.

It is almost cruel when you sleep this deeply. You know your body is getting the rest it desperately needs, but it feels as if you just fell asleep when you wake up. Like someone snapped their fingers just after you closed your eyes and immediately brought the sunlight of a new day.

Now Tuesday morning, I laid in bed and thought about the upcoming day. It would be another day working at the office. Another day of distraction through routine. I welcomed work in those first few days. It gave me a place to go and it gave me purpose. Surviving the initial days after discovering Christy's affair was all about hanging onto elements of my life where I felt my life had a purpose and where my life was valued.

However, as I mentioned earlier, my battle with panic was centered more around finding control than it was about being hopeful. I certainly did not have hope in those first days and I certainly did not have hope when I woke up on that Tuesday morning. Therefore, when I woke up after several hours of deep sleep, my only recourse was gaining a sense of control over the thoughts that came flooding in as I gained consciousness. Through the grogginess and haze of once again becoming alert, the realities of my situation flooded into the spaces that had just been filled with dreams, imagination or nothing.

I could feel the pressure building, just as it had the night before. But I did not think to write about it right then and there. This method of coping was new to me. At the time, I did not yet realize that a Moleskine notebook and a pen were my primary line of defense against panic. Instead, on that Tuesday morning, I jumped out of bed, quickly showered and threw on the first halfway decent, non-wrinkled button down shirt I could find along with the pair of jeans that were still on the floor in the same spot where I had left them the day before. I was not eating much in those first days, so I did not even think to grab something, anything, for breakfast.

I still remember that walk to work as if it were yesterday. I had forgotten to bring a jacket with me. That was how quickly I left the house. It was frigid outside, but I did not seem to feel it. Even if I did feel it, my body just did not seem to care. With each step down the street, the anxiety and panic grew. By the time I reached a traffic light about halfway to the office, I was nearing a complete breakdown. I seemed to be having every imaginable thought I could, ranging from mental images of Christy and Matt having sex the night before, to imagining the sight of Christy flushing fetal tissue down the toilet bowl after she took the Mifepristone and Misoprostol, to the question of how and when to tell the rest of my family.

I recall thinking how ridiculous I must have looked to passersby. Here was this man, walking down the streets of Denver in twenty something degree weather with no coat and tears streaming down his face. But I really did not even care. I even went as far as to internally hypothetically threaten anybody who would confront me with their opinion of my state of mind or appearance.

I thought a snap might actually help, like a quick hit of a drug to numb the pain.

Fortunately, a confrontation did not come, so I just kept on heading west towards my office. I just blankly stared ahead through waterlogged eyes. Reflecting, I should have journaled before leaving the house that morning. It would have helped with that bout of anxiety and given me a sense of control over my emotions.

Walking into work was like a blast of fresh air. I was able to gather myself and utilize the time it takes to walk through the building lobby and ride the elevator to my office to shift my focus towards the obligations of the day. In the elevator, I whipped out my cell phone and looked at my work calendar. The first half of my day was overloaded with meetings. I had about 25 minutes before I was scheduled to have a breakfast meeting to discuss the overall marketing strategy for our office. Then, I had back to back project specific meetings which were then followed up by a technical training workshop over the lunch hour. All these morning meetings meant that there were probably plenty of action items to tackle in the afternoon.

The morning seemed to fly by, and I compiled a list of all the actionable items that I would be responsible for after the slew of morning meetings. I found myself actively volunteering to take on tasks which seemed to accomplish two things. First, it meant that I did not have to hear one of my least favorite words in the business world, "voluntold," because I was just stepping up and volunteering to do something. Second, it allowed me to build an extensive list of tasks that I could distract myself with. If I could stay busy and focused on knocking out task after task, I could simply drown out any emotional distress that may hit me during the day.

The philosophy was simple. Nobody can focus on two things at once, no matter how hard we try to convince ourselves that we have this ability. By simply overwhelming my brain with a straightforward, yet extensive, to-do list, there would simply be no room for anxiety. I just would not allow it.

But stress and anxiety do not care what you will and will not allow. If the source of your panic is powerful enough, it will simply bulldoze any meager attempt to bury or avoid its existence. After my meetings, I headed back to my office to settle into my list of tasks. I had barely navigated to the network drive for the first task when a tide of terror and panic rose around me with a merciless resolve to pull me beneath the surface where reality meets the domain of fantastical torment.

This particular episode was the worst yet. It manifested in supercharged physical effects. I could feel the thumping of my heart in my chest. It was pronounced and it was extremely rapid. I grabbed my phone and enabled the feature that allows you to measure your pulse. I mentioned earlier that I am a long-distance runner and enjoy endurance activities. My normal resting heart rate, depending on the volume of my running and training, usually hovers between forty and forty-five beats per minute. My reading during this panic attack, in which I was simply sitting at my desk, skyrocketed up over one hundred and sixty beats per minute! That is about twenty beats per minute faster than my typical pulse on an intense run.

Then my respiratory rate increased. My temperature rose and sweat beads congregated on my forehead. The last domino to fall was the flood of tears pooling in my eyes. I was at work for Pete's sake! I kept telling myself to get it together. I am a manager and leader in this company. I could not let anybody see me like this.

I quickly rose from my desk and closed my office door. That would only serve to help muffle any noise, as the front wall of my office, which looks over the general work area and cubicles, is a clear glass pane. I sat back in my chair and turned away from the transparent partition. Even closing my eyes could no longer dam the impending deluge. The first tear squeezed through the crack in my eyelids. An endless stream followed.

Facing away from public view and curled around my phone which rested on my lap, I furiously typed, "how do you stop a panic attack?" I clung to one of the first suggestions, which centered around controlling your breathing and focusing your mind on a repetitive and meditative external medium. I then searched for one of the article's recommendations for meditation apps on my phone. I found one that provided several different themes for repetitive and meditative sounds.

"A beach theme! Perfect!" I thought as I stumbled through the app. It was a program that allowed you to layer different sounds on top of each other at various volumes to create the auditory environment of your choosing. First, I started with the sounds of waves crashing on the shore. In and out. In and out. Then I turned on the sound of seagulls chirping softly, reminiscent of my childhood memories of hearing the birds squawk as they cruised overhead at the Jersey shore. Next came the extremely soft horn of a tugboat, so soft that it mimicked a vessel sounding off on the edge of the horizon. Throw in a little melodic guitar and the soft pitter patter of raindrops, and the scene was set.

I am so thankful I found that app so quickly. It was transformative. I closed my eyes and just focused on the symphony of shoreline sounds. The repetitive rhythm demanded that my respiration keep time like a stubborn conductor directs his orchestra. My hyperventilating slowed until my inhales and exhales were in lockstep with the crash and subsequent recession of the waves. In and out. In and out.

With my eyes closed, I focused intensely on the scene created by the sounds streaming from my phone's speaker. The waves seemed prominent but not overly powerful. Perhaps they were two to three-foot rollers gently cascading onto the sand. The rainfall was soft and gentle, reminiscent of a day where overcast clouds and fog were draped over the ocean. The beach was empty except for the random couple walking hand in hand on the shoreline. I imagined I was sitting on a covered deck on the upper level of a beachfront house looking out at the shoreline as an occupant of the house next to mine softly strummed his guitar. It was an early morning scene where a fishing vessel had just cleared the inlet and was heading out to sea with a far-off blare of its horn.

I allowed my mind to be enveloped by this serene and peaceful departure from reality. It was almost a hypnotic dream state in which I could peer in from my reality to see myself in an alternate reality relaxing on that deck and looking out over the ocean. I started thinking about how I would pass my time on that deck if I could be transported to that exact spot at that very moment. What would I do to sort through my emotions if I could simply just exist with nothing but the breeze, the rain and the waves for company? Surely, that version of me could simply focus and think with no distractions or external demands. Picturing myself in this alternative reality gave me some much-needed clarity.

To gain control, I would have to stop avoiding my anxious thoughts, but rather write them down as a record of the irrationality of my situation. It confirmed what I had first discovered the night before. The onslaught of panic, fear and anxiety was bearing down on me and it would not be ending any time soon. It was up to me to accept this fact and arm myself to confront these perturbations with logical and reasonable thinking.

I needed to regain control of my narrative and the truth at the center of my life. My circumstances, hopes, plans and dreams were all crashing down around me. My past had turned out to be nothing more than a series of events that brought me to this dreadful moment in my life. However, even with all the destruction that surrounded me, I knew I had to take back control of who I am as a person at my core. I had to remind myself that my identity is my own and is not subject to the actions of Christy or Matt. Christy may have had control over my situation by being deceitfully evil through her affair. But I decided right then and there that she should not have any control over who I am as a man, and what I wanted my life to be going forward.

I put aside my work to-do list and resolved to focus on regaining that emotional and mental control over my life again immediately. I just knew that I could not regain focus on anything until I took that step to face the immediate threats in front of me which were swirling around in my head.

There was this nagging phrase in my mind. "Do not make a knee jerk reaction that you may regret."

I kept telling myself this over and over again. The truth is, I liked being married and I liked the fact that I had made the decision a long time ago to dedicate my life to love and partnership. That was a decision I made. Her affair did not erase the fact that I had once chosen to spend my life as a married man. Sure, it was going to make me strongly question whether I wanted to remain dedicated to a life with her. But I knew right then and there that I needed to make that decision from a place of rationality and pragmatism. I could not allow my marriage to be subject to the whims of emotional outbursts or a reactionary decision attributed to any short-term stimuli.

I decided to write down my roadmap for taking back control. Being an engineer and analytical type, I resorted to a step by step approach the best I could.

Step 1. Christy would need to tell me everything about the affair. I needed to hear every painful detail. I needed to know the timelines, feelings, and emotions of Matt and Christy's affair. I needed to know how she could possibly decide to end a baby's life behind my back and how she was able to do it so calmly. I also needed to know her reasons for deciding to betray my trust and our marriage. I needed to know if she shared private conversations or details of our married life. This was especially important to me. It did, and would continue to, bother me profusely that conversations, feelings, struggles, and intimate details of our marriage, shared between Christy and I under my perceived expectation of marital exclusivity and privacy, were being disseminated to Matt without my knowledge. It further destroyed me to think that these private details of my life with Christy were the kindling that allowed the fires of their passion to burn so vigorously.

Once Christy had told me everything. She would have to tell both her family, as well as mine. I struggled with this notion as I do believe that a husband and wife's business is their own. However, that notion is predicated on absolute trust mutually shared by both individuals within a marriage. That trust was obliterated, and Christy was solely responsible for destroying the trust I once had for her. Our families loved us and supported us. They had the same expectation of trust that Christy and I were fiercely in each other's corners. They stood by us as we promised truth and fidelity to each other almost eight years earlier. Both Christy's mother and my mother lit separate candles that Christy and I joined into one unity candle signifying the bond we promised to never break. Our families were part of all of that and I could not simply move on with Christy under the false pretense that Christy and I were still operating, uninterrupted, under the veil of that trust.

Step 2. Christy needed to relinquish any expectation of privacy from me for the foreseeable future. She had destroyed my trust in her. If I was going to fight for our marriage, then I needed to feel secure in my trust for her again. I knew it would not be healthy long term and quite honestly, pretty telling if I could not trust her without verifying and screening her messages, phone calls and emails within a certain time period. But for now, she needed to be a completely open book with me. If I wanted to see her text messages or see her phone call history, I needed to have unrestricted access. The foundation of my trust for her had been crumbled. Verification and validation were needed to rebuild that foundation.

The ability to blindly trust her again would need to be built on that foundation later.

Step 3. Christy would need to decide whether she wanted to continue to be my wife. I had to recognize and accept the fact that this was completely her decision and I did not have any control over it. I felt it was important that Christy make this decision both after telling family and friends, as well as temporarily giving up her expectations of privacy in our marriage. The reason for this is because I knew those two steps would be extremely traumatic and taxing on any fiber of a relationship that we had left. I felt that the worst thing that could happen would be for Christy to decide she wanted to continue with our marriage, only to live in misery over the next few years. If I did not feel like she had demonstrated that she was trustworthy again or I could not have an honest conversation with my loved ones about what I was truly feeling as I processed the aftermath of the affair, would our marriage just buckle under that stress? Maybe that stress would just drive her to have another affair?

Step 4. After disclosing the affair to our loved ones, working on rebuilding trust through complete transparency and Christy deciding that she wanted a marriage with me, I needed to decide if I wanted to be married to Christy. That was within my control. I needed to have the final say. What Christy did to me was not my fault and it was her decision to jeopardize everything we had ever built together. By this fact alone, I determined that it was justified and fair that I would have the final decision about the future of our relationship and marriage once I had all of the information at my disposal to make that decision.

Up until this point, decisions that profoundly affected my life were made for me without allowing me the dignity of being informed on those decisions. Christy decided to have an affair with Matt without my knowledge, leaving me to wonder why we were not connecting the way we once had. Christy bought a house and made other pivotal financial decisions with me during her affair, leaving me to make critical, risk based, decisions based on an expectation of mutual trust. All the while, she was playing a hand off to the side, actively betting against our marriage as a hedge.

Finally, Christy decided to have an abortion. My wife, the person who vowed to be true to me, terminated the potential for a new life in the interest of avoiding the inconvenience of telling me the truth. She made sure that the decision to abort the baby was made independent of her husband. Because of this, I now must live with the fact that a beautiful baby would be alive today as I am writing this. That baby would be alive today if not for Christy's selfish, secretive, senseless and destructive decision.

I had every right to own the final decision of whether Christy would be by my side as I moved forward with my life. My decisions about my life were mine to control. I may regret them, or they may not work out as planned, but they were my decisions. That is what I learned in the wake of discovering Christy's affair. Surviving is simply about doing whatever you have to do in order to navigate the imminent threat of that which you cannot control, while regaining the ability to get to work on those aspects which you can control.

I had survived the first four days of my life after discovering Christy's affair. It knocked me down and out like a sucker punch with no warning. Each subsequent discovery and revelation were like an angry mob kicking me while I laid helplessly on the ground. But after those first four days, the beating ceased. I could unfurl from a position of helplessness in the face of savagery and climb back to my feet to look out at the road ahead. I knew it would be full of curves, bumps and potholes designed to impede progress. I could not see where it ended or how treacherous it would become. But it was my road to walk down and it was time to start moving forward.

I survived.

Life Marches Forward

After those initial days of surviving the discovery of Christy's affair, I entered a new phase of the recovery period. The best way I can describe this new chapter is the "preservation" phase. As I mentioned earlier in the text, a marriage is so much more than just a relationship between two people. It is a way of life. Your marriage influences every decision you make, from the mundane, like deciding what to have for dinner on a given evening, to the pivotal, like purchasing a home, changing careers, or having a child.

The preservation phase is a slow process and has many different elements. In the two months after I discovered Christy's affair, my preservation phase was centered around preserving the marriage itself. Looking back, I do not believe it was because I actually wanted to be married to Christy anymore, but rather, because preserving that marriage meant that all of my past would not be wasted and would still be the basis of my life going forward. In a way, I would still be able to stay on the track that I had previously set out for my life.

However, after those two months, the idea of possibly salvaging any type of loving relationship became clearly unattainable. It was time for me to continue down my path alone, as the marriage itself was irretrievably broken and would only lead to unhappiness and regret moving forward. After this became clear in those initial months after discovering Christy's affair, I filed for divorce.

Even in my new life as a single man, I still felt the need to walk down the same path that I had paved before me, even if I would be doing it alone. I fought hard to preserve every other element of my life. I had worked diligently for my career, my home, my car, my athletic ability and my community. All those things were still mine, regardless of how they were tied to past decisions that I had made with Christy. In my mind, everything in my life besides my divorce was good and worthy of preservation, it was just that I had been dealt a bad hand when it came to my former marriage.

However, this notion would also be challenged. Preservation allowed me to keep an even keel with a level of familiarity and routine as one aspect of my life spun out of control all around me. But eventually, those sources of familiarity and routine came into focus as elements of a life that I had not necessarily chosen for myself. I realized that my life was still on the same path as it was before I had decided to end my marriage. I am not saying it is a bad path or the wrong path. But it hit me hard that I would not be able to truly move on until I put all that my life had become on the table and truly ask myself if a given element of my life was an element that I wanted to maintain going forward. I needed to actively choose the circumstances of my new life, not just simply carry forward elements of what my life had been.

Throughout it all, my new life has been an adventure that I never thought would be part of my story. In retrospect, I am grateful that I have this opportunity to redefine who I am and what my life will become. It has not been a smooth or easy process, but it is one that I would not give up for anything.

Since the discovery Christy's affair, I have experienced deep depths of despair and agonizing uncertainty along with the anxiety it induces. But I have also experienced the unrivaled joy of unencumbered opportunities and the hope of a better future borne out of lessons learned from my experience. I have fallen deeply in love and dealt with severe heartbreak. I have made some of the best friends I will ever have in life, while I have also drifted away from others.

Through it all, I have lived with an underlying resolve that my best days are ahead of me. My story did not end with Christy's affair. Rather, it was simply the turn of the page. Life is an amazing and wonderful gift full of unexpected twists and turns. Some of these twists and turns may lead to sadness and despair. But those wrinkles in our life story provide context and perspective for the twists and turns that produce unexpected joy and happiness beyond what we could ever have imagined.

Happiness lies in the journey, not the destination. My journey continues from here. My hopes for that journey are simple. I hope to strive to always be true to myself, and I hope to remember to always find the unmatched joy in putting others needs before my own. Finally, I hope to share my life and love with someone truly remarkable who accepts me for who I am at my core, not what she hopes I will one day become. Even when life gets complex and challenging, our love will be simple. My life's success is not rooted in material goods or money, but in a love that is everlasting and endures all things. This love is in front of me and will be the greatest love story ever told.

Key Takeaways

You will feel completely unprepared when you discover your partner's affair, and that is okay. Discovering an affair is a devastating moment. A serious relationship or marriage is predicated on complete and total trust of your partner. After discovering an affair, you may seek to convince yourself that you should have been better prepared to deal with it. This urge is founded in a fallacy. If you were even a little prepared for the moment you discovered your partner's affair, that would mean that you were not operating in complete trust of your partner and, more than likely, your relationship would have been on shaky ground already. Feeling like you are emotionally unprepared for discovering your partner's affair sucks. However, it is from a position of nobleness and truth that you are unprepared. Try to focus less on the fact that you are unprepared and instead focus on your own integrity that kept you faithful and true. At the end of the day, you will react and adapt to the situation at hand by leveraging your integrity and conscience. Your partner operated in deceit and lies. You operated in trust and love. Remember this fundamental fact, as only you will be able to look in the mirror and say to yourself, "I am a good person and I did it the right way."

Be patient with yourself in the way you chose to confront your cheating partner. You may choose to delay confronting your partner about her affair like I did, or you may simply launch into a rage where everything rushes out of you without a filter. There is no correct answer in how you choose to confront your partner after discovering her affair. Remember, she chose to have the affair, not you. She had time to make her decision to have an affair. She had time to process her feelings and emotions because of those actions.

She had time to decide to either continue with those actions or terminate them. In short, she had time that you do not. You may say things that you look back on and regret. For me personally, I felt as if I did and said a number of things that are far outside of my typical character in the immediate aftermath of discovering the affair. But remember, your reaction is not the problem. The problem is that your partner decided to betray your trust and have an affair. You were not prepared for this. Give yourself some grace as you deal with the aftermath.

Nothing you have done provides any justification for her affair. This is a tough one. A natural reaction is to Monday morning quarterback your entire marriage or relationship to try and determine how she could possibly have an affair. You may internally think back to a conversation or a moment in time when you may have not been the best husband or partner. Perhaps you can think back to a time where you zoned out while she was talking to you. Perhaps you can remember a time where you struggled to stay awake during a tough, late night conversation. Maybe there were several occasions where you did not know what to say or do to support or help her with a tough situation. There may have even been a time where you have said or done something that she found hurtful, even if that was not your intention. What makes this worse, is she may also throw these instances where you were not perfect back at you in an effort to convince you that you somehow had a hand in driving her into the arms of another man. The truth is, this is nothing more than an effort by her to deflect blame and own that she was solely responsible for her decision to have an affair. Sure, you can carry forward lessons learned for how to be a better partner. But any shortcomings you may have are not justification for her affair. Period. Intent means everything. You may have not lived up to being the perfect partner at times. But who can live up to that standard? Even in your shortcomings, your intent was always to honor the commitment you made to your partner and protect your relationship or marriage. Her intent was to dishonor her commitment to you and maliciously take advantage of your trust in her. There is simply no moral equivalency between any of your relationship shortcomings and her decision to have an affair.

You are not as alone as you may feel. In my journey, I resisted the urge to bring in family and friends for support as soon as I needed them. I felt that bringing in anybody external to my situation who had a pre-existing relationship with both me and my ex-wife would mean relinquishing the control I had over my ability to make the decisions that I would want to make about the future of my marriage. This reluctance to bring in those people in your life who genuinely love and care about you leads to extreme feelings of loneliness. Your partner cheated on you, leaving your world shattered. Shutting your family and friends out only serves to drive you further into depression. When you look to your family and friends for support, you are not relinquishing control of your ability to make the right decision for you. You are simply building a support network to provide you the understanding and confidence to make that decision for yourself. Lean on our family and friends. They will want to help you and you will be grateful to them for the rest of your life.

You will get through this. Remember who you are at your core. This affair will knock you down, but it will not knock you out. You will learn from it. You will grow from it. You will get through it. It will not be an overnight process and it will take time, but your life will be filled with joy and love again. You will come out of this as a better man. You will gain a level of insight that few will know in their lifetime. Being the victim of an affair is one of the worst experiences someone can have in his lifetime. But rising out of the lowest depth of despair often leads to the highest peaks of the human experience. You will not only get through this, but you will thrive. The best is yet to come.

If this book impacted you and your story, please leave a note about your experience as a review on Amazon!

To learn more about Sean O'Reilly or get in touch with Sean, please visit www.whenshecheatedbook.com

I wrote this book so that others going through it can find strength knowing that they are not alone. If you know someone who could benefit from reading my story or getting in touch, please share www.whenshecheatedbook.com with them.

Be Happy and Be Well!

-Sean O'Reilly

Manufactured by Amazon.ca
Bolton, ON